LATIN AMERICAN LOCAL CAPITAL MARKETS

Challenges and Solutions

Mauro Miranda, CFA, Editor

CFA Institute
Research
Foundation

Statement of Purpose

CFA Institute Research Foundation is a not-for-profit organization established to promote the development and dissemination of relevant research for investment practitioners worldwide.

Cover Image Photo Credit: PhotografiaBasica/iStock/Getty Images Plus

ISBN 978-1-944960-48-3

Editorial Staff

Mary-Kate Hines
Assistant Editor

Tracy Dinning
Senior Publishing Technology Specialist

Contents

CE Qualified Activity CFA Institute

This publication qualifies for 0.5 CE credits under the guidelines of the CFA Institute Continuing Education Program.

Biographies

Mauro Miranda, CFA, is president of CFA Society Brazil and a member of the board of trustees of CFA Institute Research Foundation. He has built his professional career in fixed income, including structured debt, and private credit. Mr. Miranda started his career in the External Debt Management Department of the Central Bank of Brazil. He then worked as a fixed-income trader and structurer, among other positions, at such firms as Bear Stearns, Lehman Brothers, and ABN AMRO in New York City, London, and São Paulo. Mr. Miranda holds bachelor's degrees in international relations and economics from the University of Brasília and an MBA from Columbia Business School. He also holds the Financial Risk Manager (FRM) designation.

Lionel Modi, CFA, is CIO of Argentina at Franklin Templeton Investments. Prior to that, he was CIO at Grupo Orígenes, one of the largest insurance companies in Argentina, and managed portfolios across a wide range of asset classes. Mr. Modi also has broad experience in pension markets, where he has held several positions on investment teams and has actively participated in and researched on behalf of many discussion boards focused on the development and growth of the Argentine capital market. He holds a bachelor's degree in economics from Universidad de Buenos Aires and a master's degree in finance from Universidad Torcuato di Tella, where he now teaches for the master in finance program.

Nicolás Álvarez, CFA, is head of the Capital Market and Financial Institutions team in the Financial Policy division of the Central Bank of Chile, where he is responsible for analyzing local and international financial market developments, institutional investor portfolios, and the regulations that affect them. He also belongs to the Technical Investment Committee (CTI) at the Superintendence of Pensions and participates in several analytical teams in the Financial Stability Committee at the Ministry of Finance of Chile. Previously, Mr. Álvarez served as portfolio manager at ING Life Insurance Company, where he was responsible for a USD 4 billion portfolio. He has taught courses on investment and risk management—most recently at Universidad de Chile—and has written several articles on these issues. Mr. Álvarez received his MS in finance from Boston College and his BA from Universidad de Chile. He also holds the FRM designation and is a member of CFA Institute and CFA Society Chile.

César Cuervo, CFA, is director of research at SURA Asset Management, where he oversees bottom-up and top-down research for investments in Latin America, both for fixed-income and listed equities. He has extensive experience in company analysis, corporate finance, and investment portfolio management. Previously, Mr. Cuervo served as director of equity research at Credicorp Capital, as asset allocation strategist and investment manager for alternative assets at Colombian pension fund BBVA Horizonte, and as investment and credit risk senior analyst at pension fund manager Porvenir, also in Colombia. He holds a BS in management from Universidad de los Andes and a master's degree in finance from the London Business School.

Jorge Unda, CFA, is CIO of Latin American asset management at BBVA Bancomer, where he is responsible for investments in Latin American funds and local investment funds in Argentina, Colombia, Peru, Chile, and Mexico. He is also director of relations with government and regulators at CFA Society Mexico. Previously, Mr. Unda served as CIO and director of third-party portfolio management in Mexico at BBVA Bancomer. He has spoken at the annual conference of Uniapravi, the annual conference of Instituto del Fondo Nacional de la Vivienda para los Trabajadores (INFONAVIT), the Securitization & Structured Finance in Latin America (SiLAS) conference, the Latin America Corporate Bond Conference, the BBVA Tokyo Seminar, GFC Mining & Investment Latin America Summit, GFC Bonds & Loans Conference, and the International Finance Conference at the Universidad Nacional Autónoma de México. Mr. Unda holds a bachelor's degree in economics from the University of the Americas Puebla and a master's degree in finance from the Instituto Tecnológico Autónomo de México.

Melvin Escudero is president of CFA Society Peru, founder and CEO of El Dorado Asset Management and El Dorado Investments, and director of the master in finance and portfolio management program at Universidad del Pacífico. He is the former regulator of the Peruvian Superintendency of Banking, Insurance and Private Pension Funds. Mr. Escudero has over 25 years of experience in the financial and capital markets.

Barbara Mainzer, CFA, is president of CFA Society Uruguay. She is an economist and currently serves as an adviser and consultant for wealth management institutions, a regular columnist at El País newspaper and TV news VTV, and a university professor of finance at Universidad Torcuato Di Tella in Buenos Aires and Universidad ORT Uruguay, where she has served as co-chair of finance as well as academic coordinator of finance. Previously, Ms. Mainzer has served as director and business manager for Julius Baer in the Southern Cone, head of Julius Baer Advisory, and vice president and Southern Cone sales manager for Merrill Lynch. She has also served on the board of directors of CFA Society Argentina & Uruguay, most recently as vice president. Ms. Mainzer is a graduate of the Program for Leadership Development at Harvard Business School.

Introduction

Economic growth depends on the efficient allocation of resources, including the two main factors of production: labor and capital. Markets, operating on each factor, have allocated these resources in economies worldwide in ways that arguably approach optimality and have fostered economic development for the benefit of billions. Capital markets, both for debt and equity securities, have allowed firms to secure funding for productive uses while providing investors with opportunities for portfolio diversification. The importance of capital markets for the development of economies and for the betterment of society cannot be overstated.

This is just as true in emerging economies with free markets, such as those found in Latin America, as it is in developed markets. However, capital markets in the region are not being utilized to the fullest. What challenges do Latin American countries face in the development of their local capital markets? How can these countries unlock the true potential of their markets and thus spur growth?

The idea behind this collection of articles is to offer a primer on the development of local capital markets in several select countries in Latin America. We discuss not only their history and current status but also their future. To this end, seven authors contributed to this project, each writing about one of seven countries: Argentina, Brazil, Chile, Colombia, Mexico, Peru, and Uruguay. Each author decided which issues they believe matter most to the progress of their local capital markets. Some authors chose a qualitative and institutional description of local markets, whereas others adopted a more quantitative approach.

Lionel Modi, CFA, provides an account of the recent evolution of capital markets in Argentina and identifies five stages in their development, culminating in the current stage that has prevailed since 2015. As Mr. Modi shows, in 2016, Argentina emerged from the international debt default status into which it fell in the early 2000s. This recovery was fundamental for attracting foreign investors to Argentina's local markets. His article discusses the main asset classes that exist in Argentina and points out that political commitment and market, tax, and pension system reforms in Argentina will be key to the future growth of its capital markets.

I discuss Brazil's equity and debt capital markets in an article that starts with a brief outline of the way these markets evolved over the past several decades. Although important advancements have occurred in the development of the country's capital markets, macroeconomic issues—including high interest rates, fiscal indiscipline, and the crowding out of private capital markets by public issuance—have constantly challenged such progress. Progress in Brazil also depends on more-efficient regulations and financial education. I argue that some of the necessary conditions for the accelerated growth and development of Brazil's capital markets are already in place, so stakeholders must take advantage of current opportunities.

Nicolás Álvarez, CFA, covers the local fixed-income market in Chile. After providing information about the characteristics of, and main players in, that market, Mr. Álvarez offers a quantitative analysis of how the market is integrated with international markets in terms of price co-movement. He also discusses recent changes in the Chilean regulatory environment and indicates that both administrative and tax reporting requirements are now friendlier to investors, especially foreign ones. Challenges that need to be tackled in Chile include the dominance of pension funds and the effect of such dominance on market liquidity and international integration.

César Cuervo, CFA, begins his article on Colombia by stating that there is ample room for growth and improvement in that country's local capital markets. He discusses several issues that are essential to making Colombian capital markets more functional and efficient. Although the local equity market is underdeveloped in terms of the ratio of market capitalization to GDP, the local fixed-income market is relatively robust and liquid, albeit more on the government side than on the corporate side. Mr. Cuervo lists stronger regulator supervision, more formalization in the economy, and better governance regarding voting and nonvoting shares—as well as other changes—as prerequisites for stronger and deeper capital markets in Colombia.

Jorge Unda, CFA, discusses Mexico's recent financial history and its impact on the development of the country's local capital markets. He acknowledges that important structural changes have taken place in the last two decades, including pension reform, the creation of a benchmark yield curve, consolidation in the banking sector, and a commitment to macroeconomic prudence. Although the crowding-out effect exists in Mexico, Mr. Unda argues that the participation of foreign investors has mitigated it. However, predicting the long-term impact of some recent reforms, including those of 2014, is difficult. For Mexico, the key to capital market development—and economic growth—seems to lie with the expansion of credit.

The recent development of the local capital markets in Peru is the theme of Melvin Escudero's article. He argues that a combination of excessive regulation, tax structure, and the predominance of banks in financing activities provides a disincentive for companies to tap the capital markets, affecting the supply side of securities. In addition, the absence of a financial culture, a preference for foreign assets, and taxes on income and capital gains on capital market securities (while bank instruments are tax exempt) have negatively affected the demand side. Given these circumstances, it is not surprising that liquidity in the Peruvian capital markets is thin. Governmental and private sector initiatives are needed to improve this scenario.

Barbara Mainzer, CFA, examines the features that make Uruguay a stable and reliable international center for business. Ms. Mainzer points out that, although the country has a long history in the financial markets, its capital markets are less developed than those of other countries in the region because of the small size of companies, corporate governance issues, and regulatory weaknesses. The primary market is more important than secondary markets, and the issuance and amount of government debt dwarf those of private debt. Still, the high-income investor base, government incentives, and increased participation of private pension funds are attractive elements that can promote the development of local capital markets in Uruguay.

Although capital markets in the countries discussed in this brief differ in their distinctive characteristics, stages of development, and relevance to the local economy, the articles collected here show that these nations share some familiar challenges, including the considerable size of the government bond markets, inadequate or insufficient regulatory oversight, and cultural characteristics that lead investors to look for investment opportunities elsewhere. The articles also share some potential solutions for promoting the accelerated development of local markets, such as economic reforms, increased regulatory efficiency, improved governance, and greater internationalization.

I hope that this publication will add to the debate on how to improve local capital markets and will encourage all stakeholders—especially issuers, investors, and regulators—to collaborate in proposing and implementing those solutions for the benefit of society.

Mauro Miranda, CFA

São Paulo, Brazil

December 2017

1. Capital Markets in Argentina: Growth and Opportunities

Lionel Modi, CFA

In the last 15 years, the Argentine local capital markets have experienced substantial change, with both the country and market going through several distinct periods. This history throws light on Argentina's present challenges as well as its prospects for the future, especially in regard to regulations and market structure.

For each period, this article discusses the characteristics of the supply of and demand for capital as various players shaped the markets. It also reviews several historically persistent features that in some cases starting in 2016 may be under reconsideration.

BRIEF CONTEXT

Argentina has a long history of institutional weakness, high inflation, and currency depreciations. As a result, the general public (retail investors) never had a culture of saving through the capital markets. They preferred to invest in real estate or in simple hard-currency holdings. High-net-worth individuals tended to hold their portfolios outside the country to avoid the institutional instability. Some of these conditions may be changing, but their lingering effects merit consideration.

Also important to note, fixed income has almost always driven the Argentine capital markets. As the data that follow show, equity has represented a small share of those markets.

A LITTLE BIT OF HISTORY

The 21st century in the history of Argentine capital markets structure divides into five subperiods. **Table 1.1** identifies these periods and summarizes them using data on the trading volume of the two biggest exchanges, the Mercado Abierto Electrónico (MAE) and the Bolsas y Mercados Argentinos (BYMA). It also presents information on the mix of equity and fixed income in the capital markets.

TABLE 1.1. YEARLY TRADING VOLUME IN ARGENTINA CAPITAL MARKETS (USD BILLIONS)

	Total			Fixed Income				Equity				Analysis Period
Years	Avg. Vol.	Year after Event Change	Rest of Period CAGR	Avg. Vol.	Year after Event Change	Rest of Period CAGR	Avg. Total Vol.	Avg. Vol.	Year after Event Change	Rest of Period CAGR	Avg. Total Vol.	
2002–2004	**36.4**	–87.7%	74.7%	**17.5**	–88.2%	73.0%	92.1%	**3.0**	–70.7%	96.1%	7.9%	Pre-sovereign restructuring
2005–2008	**132.5**	100.1	10.2	**64.7**	105.7	10.9	95.2	**6.3**	38.6	–2.5	4.8	Post-sovereign restructuring
2009–2011	**90.5**	–58.6	33.4	**44.5**	–58.9	34.9	96.3	**3.2**	–51.5	–2.4	3.7	Post-pension funds
2012–2015	**151.1**	–0.4	17.3	**74.9**	0.9	17.1	98.3	**2.6**	–47.8	33.4	1.7	Currency and capital controls
2016–	**324.3**	81.4		**320.0**	82.5		98.7	**4.3**	23.7		1.3	Present

Note: CAGR is compound annual growth rate.

Sources: Author analysis, Instituto Argentino de Mercado de Capitales, and Mercado Abierto Electrónico.

2002–2004: PRE-SOVEREIGN RESTRUCTURING

At the end of 2001, Argentina was navigating through a default on its sovereign debt and was still absorbing the effects of a large currency depreciation. Until 2004, the fixed-income market was growing significantly, but trading volumes were low because a large proportion of sovereign and corporate debt was in default. Equities were experiencing the highest level of total share of volume traded in the series, but this situation was mainly a result of the depressed fixed-income market. The supply of capital was led by pension funds, primarily the Administradora de Fondos de Jubilaciones y Pensiones (AFJPs), followed by insurance companies with pension-like obligations. These entities continued to receive inflows as economic activity started to recover. Mutual funds were active, mostly in the equity and cash management markets. Fixed-income funds suffered heavy redemptions because of the sovereign debt default.

Corporate bonds were not widely issued from 2001 through 2004 because they were going through their own restructuring processes. Some local sovereign debt was issued, mainly linked to inflation, and some other denominated in hard currency. The central bank also issued short-term marketable instruments to implement monetary policy.

2005–2008: POST-SOVEREIGN RESTRUCTURING

The majority of the sovereign debt-restructuring process was completed in 2005, marking the end of the first subperiod.[1] As Table 1.1 shows, from 2005 through 2008, total trading volume doubled, driven by fixed income. From then on, equity started to gradually lose share. The major suppliers of capital continued to be pension funds, which drove growth both in trading and in the size of the mutual fund industry. Throughout this period, the entire local capital market continued to grow, with the pension fund industry responsible for almost all of that growth.

On the demand side, the government and central bank continued tapping the fixed-income market. Both provincial and corporate debt started to be more active. In the equity market, some successful IPOs appeared and trading volume was stable. Both seasoned and newly issued bonds were diversified across maturity and credit risk levels. Demand existed for both short-term and long-term assets.

2009–2011: POST-PENSION FUNDS

The second event that dramatically changed the Argentine local capital markets occurred at the end of 2008, shortly after the US subprime mortgage crisis. The

[1]I state *majority* because there was still a minor (but not negligible) portion of the defaulted debt that remained under *holdout* status. This situation, not completely solved until 2016 as will be seen, imposed on the sovereign several difficulties and restrictions in tapping global markets because of litigations.

Argentine pension system suddenly changed with the dissolution of private pension funds and the establishment of a state-controlled pay-as-you-go system. The money that previously belonged to the various private pension funds was consolidated into one fund, the Fondo de Garantía de Sustentabilidad (FGS), which had a different investment approach than its predecessors. The FGS was more oriented to financing public infrastructure than to diversified investing in capital markets. Questions arose as to whether it should be managed as a complement of the pay-as-you-go system becoming more passive and cash management oriented. Also, regulation forced the fund's equity holdings to be kept in a portfolio without any further trading. This requirement greatly reduced market depth. Thus, in this period, the Argentine capital market experienced a huge reduction in depth and liquidity and fell into a deep rethinking and reinvention period because its main source of funding—pension funds—had disappeared.

Table 1.2 compares the 2005–08 period with 2009–2011. The assets under management (AUM) of market-oriented institutional investors dropped sharply, a change that also reduced total trading volume in the latter period, as Table 1.1 shows. Insurance companies became the biggest players, and they had very different investment needs (almost entirely fixed income) and time horizons from pension funds. Apart from the few remaining annuity and retirement firms—most of them leftovers from the former pension system—the insurance market had very short-term liabilities, so demand for long-term assets became scarce.

Mutual funds began to seek new clients and found fresh prospects in the corporate sector. Companies started to explore techniques for cash management optimization through mutual funds, a practice they had not frequently followed in the past. A notable driver in this process was sluggish private sector credit demand, which did not give much incentive for banks to try to capture those excess cash balances. As a result, institutional demand for assets became more short term and focused almost exclusively on fixed-income securities. Equity found few local buyers.

The demand for capital also adapted to this new environment. More companies started to offer short-term debt similar to commercial paper. From time to time, companies explored longer terms to maturity. For the most part, the state issued floating-rate debt with maturities no longer than five years.

2012–2015: CURRENCY & CAPITAL CONTROLS

The next event to transform the capital markets was the implementation of both currency and capital controls at the end of 2011 and beginning of 2012. **Table 1.3** presents details for the relevant players.

TABLE 1.2. MAIN MARKET-ORIENTED INSTITUTIONAL INVESTORS AUM EVOLUTION, 2005–2011* (USD BILLIONS)

	Post-Sov. Restructuring (2005–2008)				Post-Pension Funds (2009–2011)			
Investor	Avg. Vol.	Year after Event Change	Rest of Period CAGR	Avg. Total Vol.	Avg. Vol.	Year after Event Change	Rest of Period CAGR	Avg. Total Vol.
Pension funds	**24.2**	20.3%	5.4%	68.7%				
Insurance companies	**8.7**	20.7	13.6	24.9	**11.8**	6.9%	6.7%	73.4%
Mutual funds—FGS					**0.8**	n/a	22.5	5.0
Mutual funds**	**2.2**	197.1	16.9	6.4	**3.5**	31.3	7.7	21.6
Total	**35.2**	24.4	8.2		**16.1**	-58.4	7.7	

*FGS not included for reasons discussed previously. Only mutual fund holdings in the FGS portfolio are considered.

**Excludes pension fund and insurance companies' holdings to avoid double counting.

Sources: Author analysis, (former) Superintendencia de AFJPs, Superintendencia de Seguros de la Nación, Cámara Argentina de Fondos Comunes de Inversión, and FGS.

As Table 1.3 shows, these economic controls represented an unfortunate increase in the level of financial repression. Nevertheless, the impact on the local capital markets was positive because the controls increased awareness of the markets as a tool for both saving and diversification. As Table 1.1 shows, trading volume expanded at a good pace throughout this period. Reinforcing the critical status of the currency market in this period was the fact that a significant part of the volume increase could be just explained by trading strategies that sought solely to trade hard currency through a combination of market transactions.

Table 1.3 reveals another important feature of the markets. The category of "Mutual funds—others" includes mainly corporations' treasury investments and, to a lesser degree, professional associations' pension pools that continued to exist after the 2008 pension system reform. Corporations played a key role in the evolution of "Mutual

TABLE 1.3. MAIN MARKET-ORIENTED INSTITUTIONAL INVESTORS AUM EVOLUTION, 2012–2017* (USD BILLIONS)

	FX Restrictions (2012–2015)				Present (2016–2017/1Q)				– (2017/2Q)	
Investor	Avg. Vol.	Year after Event Change	Rest of Period CAGR	Avg. Total Vol.	Avg. Vol.	Year after Event Change	1Q 2017 Change	Avg. Total Vol.	Vol.	QoQ Chg. %
Insurance companies	**12.2**	-9.7%	10.0%	61.0%	**18.7**	19.2%	13.1%	48.8%		
Mutual funds—FGS	**1.0**	-16.6	15.9	5.1	**2.3**	9.1	123.9	6.0		
Mutual funds—retail	**0.7**	3.7	10.9	3.4	**3.2**	217.2	50.0	8.3	**5.7**	49.0
Mutual funds—others **	**6.1**	-2.7	38.4	30.5	**14.2**	22.9	43.7	36.9		
Total	**20.0**	-5.1	17.8		**38.4**	26.1	31.3			

*FGS not included for reasons discussed previously; only its mutual funds holdings considered.

**Excludes insurance companies' holdings to avoid double counting.

Sources: Author analysis, Cámara Argentina de Fondos Comunes de Inversión, Superintendencia de Seguros de la Nación, and FGS.

funds—others" by providing funding to the market as they continuously increased their cash management activities through mutual fund investing because financial restrictions were causing obstacles in paying dividends

Continuing the trend that started during the previous period, short-term fixed-income instruments led the growth in trading volume. All types of short-term debt and structured products experienced increased issuance. In addition, two asset classes that were previously almost nonexistent emerged during this period and dominated the scene. First, led by the state and the provinces, local-currency-denominated US dollar-linked bonds became very popular.[2] Second, currency futures grew exponentially in trading volume.

2016–PRESENT

The fifth period began with the change in political regime at the end of 2015. Economic and financial measures at that time radically modified previous standings in a wide range of areas. Argentina finally declared the end of its default status that began in 2001 by closing all of the still-pending holdout litigations. It announced its reopening to international financial markets, put into place a successful tax amnesty, and started working vigorously toward modernizing and developing its local capital market. As can be seen in Table 1.1, trading volume skyrocketed (more than doubling between 2015 and 2016). International investors actively traded Argentine bonds, and this new external flow provided an opportunity for the local market, led by the state, to start issuing new debt—in both hard currency and local currency—for short and long maturities. For the first time in Argentina's history, a local-currency fixed-rate bond curve was created. Corporations and the provinces followed that trend. On the equity side, some IPOs and secondary offerings were successfully placed.

Table 1.3 reveals a new set of players as a local source of funding: high-net-worth and other retail investors. These entrants emerged as a result of the tax amnesty and the emerging capital market reforms discussed later. The last columns of Table 1.3 show the rise of retail mutual funds' AUM.

Another notable change occurred in this last period. As detailed in **Table 1.4**, the dominance of cash management funds in the mutual fund sector appears to show signs of reversal. This development could change the supply of funds observed for the last eight years since the dissolution of private pension funds.

[2]These bonds are issued in local currency, but their principal is fixed in US dollars. As a result, each of the bond cash flows is computed in US dollars, but it's settled in local currency using the corresponding FX rate at time of payment.

TABLE 1.4. CASH VS. ASSET MANAGEMENT MUTUAL FUND AUM

	FX Restrictions		Present		
Strategy	2014	2015	2016	1Q 2017	2Q 2017
Cash management	**54.5%**	**56.0%**	**53.5%**	**55.0%**	**48.0%**
Change		*2.8*	*–4.5*	*2.8*	*–12.7*
Asset management	**45.5%**	**44.0%**	**46.5%**	**45.0%**	**52.0%**
Change		*–3.3*	*5.7*	*–3.2*	*15.6*

Sources: Author analysis, Cámara Argentina de Fondos Comunes de Inversión, and Comisión Nacional de Valores.

CURRENT SITUATION

This history should alert the reader to the general structural facts that are key to understanding the Argentine capital markets:

1. a large (but decreasing) bias toward cash management and other short-term investment practices,

2. a strong focus on fixed income,

3. a small but growing use of derivatives (especially currency futures),

4. a lagging equity market,

5. a retail investing sector that is growing rapidly because of a successful tax amnesty,

6. the absence of a private, fully funded pension system, and

7. a poor culture of saving through the capital markets.

Two additional elements are noteworthy: (1) low penetration of technology (but much work is being done in this matter) and (2) the recent demutualization of BYMA (the most important stock exchange), which has established a modern platform for the future growth of the equity market and positions Argentina to connect with its regional peers' markets.

An important recent factor in the fixed-income market is an increasing number of bond issuances of longer maturities and of different types—notably, a 10-year fixed-rate local-currency sovereign issue. The key factor in this issuance was international investors, which have been providing strong demand for Argentine assets since the 2015 presidential election. This demand provides new buyers and a solid base for the transition that the Argentine capital markets are experiencing.

MARKET INSTRUMENTS

With this setup in mind, I will now swiftly summarize the available market instruments because I believe they are the final product of the interaction between all these market-intrinsic features.

EQUITY

The main investors in equity are mutual funds and, increasingly, retail and high-net-worth individuals. Liquidity is concentrated on the "Merval" and "Merval Argentina" stock indexes. Recent IPOs and secondary (follow-on) offerings consist primarily of stocks that are also listed in foreign markets to leverage that demand. At the time of this writing, Argentina is still being considered a "frontier market" by MSCI, but that status is expected to change to "emerging market" in the near future.

FIXED INCOME

Local currency.

Because of inflation and macroeconomic instability, local-currency bonds are dominated by short to medium maturities. The following is a list of available subclasses together with their most popular issuers:

- Inflation-linked bonds: sovereign, quasi-sovereigns
- US dollar-linked bonds: sovereign, provinces, corporates
- Floater bonds/bills:
    - Badlar rate: sovereign, provinces, corporates
    - Monetary policy rate: sovereign
- Fixed-rate bonds: sovereign, corporates

- Pure discount bills: sovereign, central bank, sub-sovereigns
- Fideicomisos financieros[3]: corporates

Hard currencies.

These bonds provide a wide range of maturities, mainly in US dollars and euros:

- Fixed-rate bonds: sovereign, provinces, corporates
- Argentine peso-linked bonds[4]: corporates

DERIVATIVES

The derivatives market is still not very developed. Instruments are mostly futures, with currency and soybeans as the underlying assets. Institutional investors and bank regulations are not friendly to this asset class. Also, a legal framework for netting is not in place.

REMAINING CHALLENGE

As previously stated, since the 2015 presidential elections up to the time of this writing, international investors have been the main providers of funding in the Argentine markets. Now, the main challenge is that the Argentine local market, which has been lagging for years, needs to deepen and increase—not only in general size but also in the diversity of its investment profiles and issuers. Some changes are already taking place (e.g., the rise in retail and high-net-worth investors), but many more are needed. Regulatory improvements and other market-oriented structural reforms should be established to achieve this goal.

THE WAY FORWARD

The local capital market is currently the subject of strategic discussion in Argentina. Much work is being done, and political commitment regarding the market's development is strong. The changes under discussion will unlock the market's potential and are key to its future. The following subsections summarize the most relevant changes.

---

[3]Basically unleveraged asset-backed securities. They've proven to be very robust instruments over time, even during 2001 crises.

[4]Identical to US dollar-linked bonds, but the opposite way. Bonds are issued and payments are settled in US dollars, but the underlying principal is fixed in Argentine pesos.

REFORMS.

Many regulatory changes are being studied and discussed on the political front.

Capital market reform.

Some key actions of reform are as follows:

1. Speed up and improve the efficiency of the filing processes for public offerings (e.g., help small-cap and microcap companies).
2. Provide new types of funds/mutual funds (such as funds of funds, locally listed exchange-traded funds, and private equity).
3. Improve mutual fund regulations.
4. Provide new distribution channels and legal vehicles (such as local private banking).
5. Update regulations regarding market trading (e.g., market making and repos as a form of short-term borrowing for dealers in government securities).
6. Establish a derivatives netting framework.

Tax system reform.

Aimed mainly at the general economy, these reforms are intended to reduce distortions and inefficiencies in the tax system but also include some items that could be important to the future of the local capital market and its practices—namely, tax incentives for long-term savings (e.g., a voluntary pension savings system) and inheritance taxation (not currently in place in Argentina).

Pension system reform.

A general discussion is underway about the current pay-as-you-go system, the future of FGS, and the creation of a private, voluntary savings pension system with tax benefits.

TRENDS.

Some current regulations are already changing and are expected to change further.

Tax amnesty spillover.

In March 2017, the end of the biggest tax amnesty in Argentine history (which began at the end of 2016) was announced, with a total amount of USD 116.8 billion declared.

In addition to its impact on national fiscal accounts, the amnesty was also important for the future development of the local capital market because (a) about 80% of that amount was invested outside Argentina and some of that money is expected to come back to the local capital market, and (b) this new declared capital is expected to locally create additional wealth. In any case, the result should be a boost in the private banking and asset management businesses.

Technological change.

The stock exchanges are investing heavily in technology so they can scale up to meet the projected growth in trading volume. Research is also being carried out using real-time technology for risk assessment, and suitable infrastructure is being developed to support automated and algorithmic trading.

Small-cap and microcap financing.

In the last several years, many regulatory changes have been made to encourage the financing of small-cap and microcap businesses because they form the base of the Argentine economy. Growth in this sector, both in the number of businesses and in the volume of tradable instruments, is expected.

CONCLUSION

Table 1.5 provides perspective on how the Argentine equity market compares with its regional peers. These comparative data suggest the growth potential of Argentina.

As Table 1.5 shows, in 2016, both the size and liquidity of Argentina's local equity market were still remarkably small. Total market capitalization at USD 63.4 billion represents a mere 13% of GDP (4% if only free float is considered). The trading volume total of just USD 4.3 billion implies a share turnover rate below 7%. The numbers in almost every measure are well below that of Argentina's peer group. Thus, Argentina has a wide array of opportunities.

Unlocking this potential is the challenge for the local capital market. If structural reforms and regulatory improvements gather momentum, these indicators can be expected to increase manyfold. A long road remains to be traveled, but Argentina has already started putting its regulatory and structural matters in order and has the conviction and willingness to continue moving forward.

TABLE 1.5. EQUITY MARKET SELECTED INDICATORS FOR ARGENTINA'S LATIN AMERICAN PEERS, 2016

	Argentina	Peru	Colombia	Chile	Mexico	Brazil
Market capitalization (USD billions)	63.4	80.1	103.4	209.9	333.5	774.1
Market capitalization (% of GDP)	13%	42%	37%	85%	32%	43%
Trading volume (USD billions)	4.3	3.1	14.1	24.8	106.4	572.6
Trading volume (% of GDP)	1%	2%	5%	10%	10%	32%
Share turnover	7%	4%	14%	12%	32%	74%
Number of listed companies	100	217	68	214	137	338

Sources: World Federation of Exchanges, Instituto Argentino de Mercado de Capitales, and the World Bank.

2. Equity and Fixed-Income Capital Markets in Brazil: Moving Forward

Mauro Miranda, CFA

BACKGROUND

The history of Brazil's capital markets is the history of the development, over the past six decades, of the country's financial institutions (governmental and privately-owned), its laws and regulations, and its economy at large. A few institutions that specialized in the placement of equity securities had been active since the 1940s, but proper investment banks did not exist in Brazil until the mid-1960s.[5] Initially, the Central Bank of Brazil, created in 1964, was tasked with various activities related to supervising the country's capital markets. But it was only in 1976, with the creation of the Comissão de Valores Mobiliários (CVM),[6] that the regulation and supervision of those markets became concentrated into one governmental entity.

Although the basic legal and regulatory environment was mostly in place by the late 1980s, two prerequisites for the growth of capital markets did not exist until the early to mid-1990s: a higher level of openness in the economy, which attracted greater foreign investment, and the macroeconomic stability brought by "Plano Real," a set of hyperinflation-curbing economic measures that included the introduction of a new currency.

Until just two decades ago, the supply of equity and debt instruments in Brazil's capital markets was quite limited. Because Brazil was a relatively closed economy until the late 1980s, there was little need for companies to access capital markets (even if demand for securities existed) because capital expenditures were low. Firms' own resources and retained earnings, as well as subsidized funding from government agencies, met most, if not all, such expenditures.[7] The role of the Brazilian National Bank for Economic and Social Development in offering cheap funding to local companies—although arguably essential for promoting the country's economic development—has historically hindered the full development of the local capital markets. Additionally, the significant industrialization of the country in the 1950s and 1960s was led by several state-owned

[5]Costa (2006).

[6]Brazil's Securities and Exchange Commission.

[7]See an interesting historical discussion in Mendonça de Barros (2000).

enterprises (many of which were later privatized) with direct access to government funding. Still, some of these large, state-owned companies did access the capital markets and for an extended period dominated them, representing a substantial portion of the trading volume in the local stock exchanges.

The last two decades saw impressive growth in the activity of local capital markets in Brazil, both in equity and in debt instruments. In the equity markets, the São Paulo Stock Exchange became one of the top 20 exchanges in the world, with a market capitalization of USD 955 billion at the end of 2017.[8] The Novo Mercado, introduced in 2000, has attracted an increasing number of investors as companies listed in this segment must follow stricter corporate governance standards than those required by law. In the debt markets, public interest in debentures (local corporate bonds) picked up over time as investment funds dedicated to credit began to emerge. More recently, a special instrument called an "infrastructure debenture" came into vogue with individual investors because of the tax benefits offered to them. Regulation of public offerings of debt and equity securities was consolidated under CVM's Instrução 400/03 almost 15 years ago and has been regularly reviewed for improvement by CVM, providing a high standard of safety for investors. This safety is based on the large amount of information companies must disclose before selling their securities in the capital markets.

Figure 2.1 shows the evolution of debt and equity capital markets issuance in Brazil over the last 12 years. The dip in issuance observed from 2014 to 2015 is largely the result of the depreciation of the Brazilian real versus the US dollar, but issuance volume decreased in 2015–2016 mostly because of the high-interest-rate environment, as I discuss in the next section. In local currency terms, issuance levels in 2017 were in line with those observed in 2012–2013.

Despite great improvement over the decades, Brazil's capital markets have a long way to go in terms of growth and development. Next, I discuss some of the challenges faced by the equity and debt capital markets in Brazil and note some of the changes necessary for further growth.

CHALLENGES

Although the growth of local capital markets in Brazil has been noticeable over the past decades as measured by both issuance volume and number of participants (including issuers and investors), many factors still contribute to the relative underdevelopment of these markets. These factors include economic, regulatory, and cultural characteristics

[8]World Federation of Exchanges (2017).

FIGURE 2.1. LOCAL CAPITAL MARKETS NEW ISSUANCE IN BRAZIL, 2006–2017

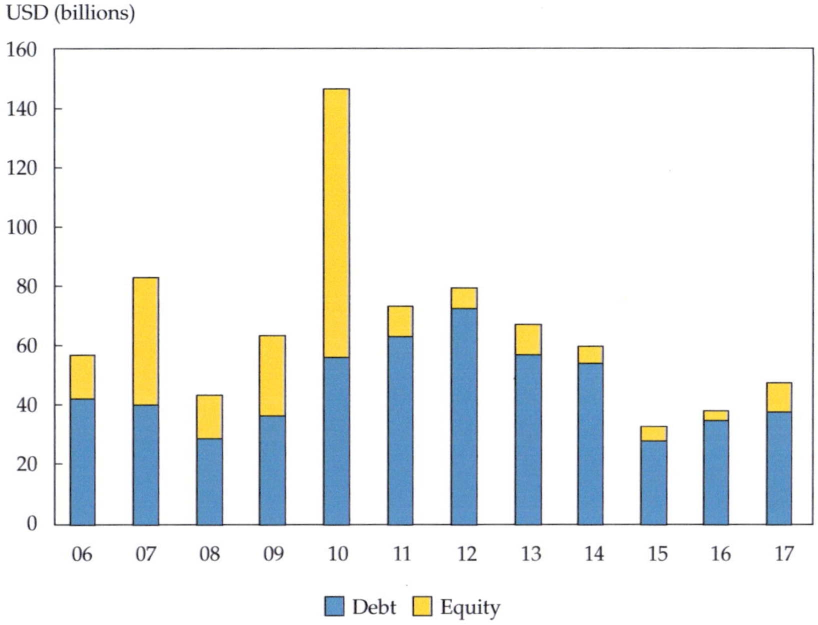

Note: 2017 data as of 30 November.

Source: ANBIMA (2017). ANBIMA is the Brazilian Financial and Capital Markets Association, a self-regulatory organization.

that have adversely affected growth in the number and market capitalization of equity and debt new issues in the country.

One major challenge to the development of both equity and debt capital markets has been the comparatively high interest rates that Brazil has offered to investors through National Treasury notes and bonds. Since the macroeconomic stabilization of the mid-1990s, the inflation rate has been kept mostly in check—especially compared with the days of hyperinflation before the Plano Real—but it is still relatively high. On average, inflation has exceeded 6% per year over the last decade (the rate observed in 2017, below 3%, being a notable exception). In addition, the elevated financing needs of the public sector and the subsequent deterioration of government finances, with persistent fiscal deficits during the last four years, have contributed to keeping interest rates high. An administration whose ideological persuasion was more politically populist than economically sound heavily promoted an expansionary fiscal policy from 2010 to 2016. Consequently, the inflation rate stood well above the target pursued by the

Central Bank of Brazil, forcing its Monetary Policy Committee to adopt a tight stance despite a continued countrywide clamor for lower interest rates.

The historically high level of interest rates in Brazil is one of the damaging results of a classic crowding-out effect. As the central government must increasingly borrow to meet its needs and obligations, private savings are used for purchasing government bonds instead of financing investment spending. To attract local investors as the outstanding amount of debt increases, government bonds must pay high interest rates that are commensurate with both (1) returns that could possibly be obtained from other (albeit riskier) investments and (2) the higher inflation risk incurred as the amount of national debt increases.[9] Although Brazil is open to foreign portfolio investment, which could mitigate the crowding-out effect, the interest rate differential between local and foreign government bonds has been kept relatively high to entice nonresidents to finance the government deficit. The consequence for local capital markets is clear: With a lower level of investment spending, firms have less need to tap the capital markets to raise financing and instead focus on obtaining funding from traditional sources, such as financial institutions and development banks.

Figure 2.2 displays the evolution of nominal and interest rates in Brazil over the last two decades. The annual nominal interest rate is measured as the accumulated daily average returns paid by government bonds,[10] while the real interest rates shown are the nominal rate for each year minus inflation.[11] Annual nominal interest rates in the 1996–2003 period were in the 17% to 29% range. In the following years, they fell into the 8% to 19% range—still quite high (albeit on a consistent downward trend) compared with rates seen in developed economies.

Given this situation, it is unsurprising that, in Brazil, institutional and individual investors alike have preferred government debt[12] to equity and debt instruments that carry risks. On the demand side of the capital markets equation, investors have naturally shunned equity and corporate debt markets in favor of financing the public debt because of the opportunity to invest in government bonds that pay high interest rates and involve zero credit risk. The Tesouro Direto program, created in 2002 (similar to the TreasuryDirect program offered by the US Department of the Treasury), has made investing in government bonds even easier. Investors can purchase fractions of bonds with values as small as BRL 30 (approximately USD 9). It is difficult for capital market products to compete with these investments, and

[9]If the amount of debt becomes unwieldy, the central government could, in theory, be forced to print money to repay its obligations, which would most likely cause inflation.

[10]Known as Taxa SELIC.

[11]Inflation is measured by the changes in the IPCA (Índice Nacional de Preços ao Consumidor Amplo), Brazil's official price index.

[12]Data compiled by Abrapp (Brazilian Association of Pension Funds) in August 2017 indicate that almost 71% of the aggregate portfolios of all pension funds in Brazil are invested in government bonds or fixed-income funds (which invest primarily in government bonds). Equities represent less than 18% of that combined portfolio, and only 2.8% of all investments are directed to corporate debt. See Abrapp (2017).

FIGURE 2.2. NOMINAL VS. REAL INTEREST RATES IN BRAZIL, 1996–2017

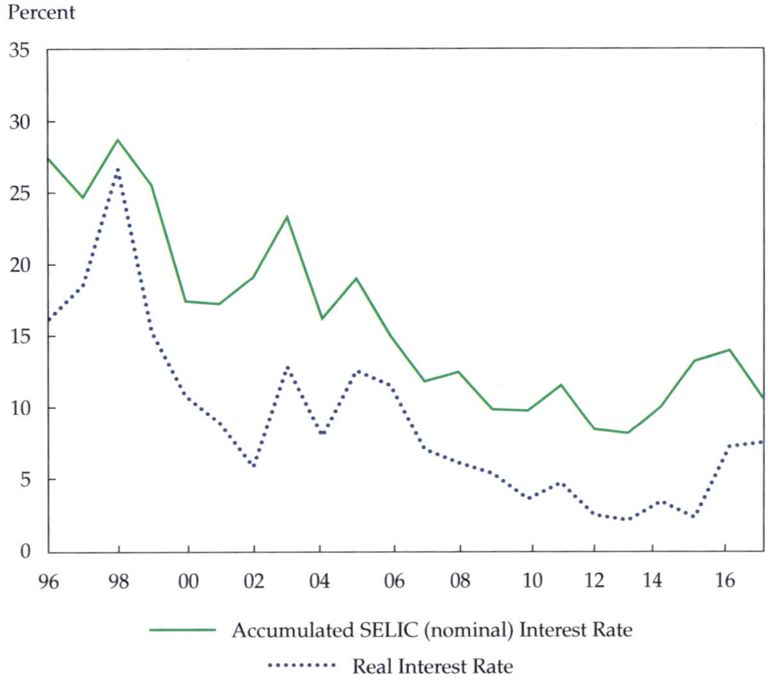

Note: 2017 data as of November.

Sources: Central Bank of Brazil and IBGE (Brazilian Institute of Geography and Statistics).

the National Treasury is certainly not shy about marketing its bonds.[13] The combination of high interest rates, zero credit risk, and the active promotion of government debt by the National Treasury makes these bonds quite attractive to local investors. The consequence of this combination for the local capital markets in Brazil is reflected in the number of investors: Almost 1.8 million individual investors are registered to transact with government bonds in the Tesouro Direto program,[14] whereas only 613,000 individuals have brokerage accounts for investing in stocks on the local stock exchange.[15]

[13]The Tesouro Direto website (www.tesouro.fazenda.gov.br/tesouro-direto) goes beyond informing investors about government bonds and actively promotes the purchase of these instruments by stating that individual investors "earn more" and "have the same return as large investors" when they invest in government bonds.

[14]Tesouro Nacional (2017).

[15]B3 (2017). The growth over the last decade and a half, however, has been significant: The number of individual investors with brokerage accounts in Brazil was approximately 85,000 in 2002; 219,000 in 2006; 611,000 in 2010; and 564,000 in 2014.

For individual investors, buying debt products issued by financial institutions, such as *certificados de depósito bancário* (known as CDBs and similar to the certificates of deposit offered by US banks), is also a common practice. Even though these instruments carry the credit risk of the issuer, two factors make them the most popular fixed-income product among Brazilian investors. First, they usually offer returns in line with those on government bonds with similar maturities because their interest rate is typically linked to the interbank interest rate,[16] which, in turn, is close to the average return on government bonds. Second, the Fundo Garantidor de Créditos (FGC) insures deposits of up to BRL 250,000 (approximately USD 75,000) per individual investor and per financial conglomerate.[17] Considering that according to Central Bank of Brazil data 99.7% of all Brazilian investors exposed to banks' credit risk currently have holdings that are fully insured by the FGC, it is little wonder individual investors favor bank paper over stocks and corporate bonds. The figures seem to back this assertion: Although individual investors hold BRL 167 billion (approximately USD 50 billion) in shares at the São Paulo Stock Exchange,[18] the total outstanding amount of CDBs is BRL 629 billion (approximately USD 189 billion).[19]

Another challenge relates to laws and regulations that apply to capital markets. Such regulations play a fundamental role in how and at what pace such markets can develop in an economy, which is certainly the case in Brazil. The willingness and ability of issuers and investors alike to sell and buy equity and debt securities is a function of how easy it is to participate in the capital markets and how fair participants think such markets are. In Brazil, financial regulation is based on highly detailed rules that must be followed to the letter, lest, for instance, the regulator turn down a public offering of new securities.

With excessive regulation, the cost of compliance for companies accessing the capital markets is quite high, a situation that has motivated firms to look for bank debt and for (cheaper) funding from such official sources as development banks. As a byproduct of overregulation and extremely specific rules for company disclosures and public offerings, redundant and conflicting norms have inevitably appeared and have negatively affected issuers' interest in and ability to tap the capital markets. On the demand side, investors tend to be warier of investing in securities (especially equities) when instances of unethical or criminal behavior—including improper disclosure, front running, insider trading, and outright fraud—come to light. Excessive and ineffective regulation, combined with insufficient enforcement of existing laws and rules, have discouraged greater participation of firms and investors in capital markets in Brazil.

---

[16]The Brazilian interbank deposit rate is called Taxa DI.

[17]The FGC in Brazil performs a role similar to that of the Federal Deposit Insurance Corporation (FDIC) in the United States. As per FGC's rules, individual investors have their deposits insured for a total aggregate amount of BRL 1 million (approximately USD 300,000) over a four-year period.

[18]B3 (2017).

[19]According to Cetip statistics, available at www.cetip.com.br.

A third challenge to the development of capital markets is the level of financial education among Brazilian investors. Even among investors who are educated enough to understand the importance of saving, few people understand the benefits of diversification and the way financial products (other than government bonds and bank paper) work. Macroeconomic conditions and the regulatory environment are partly responsible for this. Macroeconomic conditions include high interest rates, which make it less desirable for investors to look for investments other than government bonds and secured bank paper (thus reducing the demand for capital market securities). Regulation, for its part, has played a role in discouraging firms from diversifying their sources of funding (thus negatively affecting the supply of capital market securities).

Given this situation, education about financial products hardly seems a necessity: Investors have been able to earn a fair return without having to subject themselves to the ups and downs of the stock market or to the credit risk present in corporate debt, even if securities in this market offer a higher return. But without sufficient funding for productive activities in the private sector, economic growth is held back, affecting future income and living standards. Hence, the challenge is that the low level of financial education about capital market securities is detrimental to the entire country, not just to individuals in their role as investors.

Other challenges to the development of local capital markets in Brazil exist, and this coverage is by no means exhaustive. In the equity markets, one common deterrent to investment is caution regarding minority shareholders' rights and the reduction of returns caused by the actions of controlling shareholders.[20] In fixed-income markets, excessive technicity has added yet another layer of unnecessary complication and transaction costs for market participants.[21] Both markets have also been negatively affected by the subsidized credit offered by development banks, which creates distortions in the risk–return relationship and helps worsen the government's fiscal position. And these are just a few examples. What must be done, then, to get the local capital markets in Brazil on the track to growth and development?

LOOKING AHEAD

Brazilian issuers and investors, as well as the economy itself, stand to benefit from increased diversification of funding sources and investment alternatives. Several conditions and initiatives must be present for such development to become a reality. None of them is sufficient on its own; they are all necessary if Brazil is to have more robust capital markets.

[20]Matos (2017) discusses the impact of higher standards of governance for minority shareholders.

[21]See Miranda (2017).

First and most important, the development of capital markets in Brazil depends on macroeconomic stability with low to moderate interest rates. As long as government bonds continue to absorb a large proportion of private sector savings and offer a significant return at zero credit risk, equities and corporate debt will have little chance to take off in a meaningful way. At the time of writing, Brazil is experiencing its lowest level of interest rates in recent history, and investors are being forced to look at risky assets in their search for yield, affecting positively the demand for securities issued in equity and debt capital markets. But such low rates will only be sustainable if the government controls spending and addresses the fiscal deficit. Additionally, much-needed reforms, including the reform of the social security system, must be approved by the Brazilian Congress. In the long run, this is a prerequisite for the country to enjoy a low-interest-rate environment for longer and for the creation of favorable conditions for business—and, consequently, capital market—growth. The opportunity currently afforded by low-to-negative global interest rates and low domestic inflation must not be wasted.

Second, changing and modernizing laws and regulations, as well as increasing effective enforcement, will be crucial in attracting more issuers and investors to Brazil's local capital markets. As the main capital markets regulator, CVM will play a major role in this regard. It is reassuring to see that CVM has recently begun a series of interactions with market participants to identify ways to streamline capital market regulations and reduce the cost of compliance. To be sure, regulators must implement and defend investor protection without creating disincentives for the actual development of the markets themselves. Part of the answer to this challenge will come from the intelligent use of regulatory technology (or RegTech) to improve regulatory processes.[22] Also, effective enforcement of market regulation creates a sense of security for investors and other market participants but is dependent on the ability of the regulator to impose heavy fines in the case of misconduct or criminal behavior. A recent step in the right direction was increasing the maximum fine that CVM could impose from BRL 250,000 (approximately USD 75,000) to BRL 250 million (approximately USD 75 million). This change has created a negative incentive for potential wrongdoers and has helped boost trust in the markets.

Third, the level of financial education among current and potential investors needs to be improved. Unquestionably, one aspect of financial education that must be promoted is the culture of saving and financial planning, so that investors can better understand budget constraints and intertemporal choices. But financial education must move beyond that and provide information to the public about (1) the variety of financial products that are available and how they work, (2) the role of capital markets in supplying such products and the importance of the markets in providing opportunities for

[22]Arner, Barberis, and Buckley (2017, p. 16) point out that "the primary barrier to RegTech's development is not technological limitations but, rather, the ability of regulators to process the large volumes of data that the technology itself generates."

diversification in investment portfolios, and (3) investors' ability to diversify through investment in securities issued in the equity and debt capital markets as a means of achieving long-term goals. The initiatives put in place by regulators and self-regulatory organizations[23] are fundamental to attaining higher levels of financial education and must be continued and improved. Also, financial education, at least on a basic level, must be made a mandatory course in secondary education as students prepare to enter adulthood and face financial decisions. Fourth and finally, financial institutions must promote investor education more broadly—and those operating under an "open architecture" approach are better positioned to do so while keeping interests aligned, allowing investors to make choices that are better informed.

These developments and initiatives will undoubtedly improve the state of Brazilian equity and debt capital markets and take them to a level approaching that achieved in the most advanced countries. One overarching goal is to increase the number of investors participating in such markets. According to the Receita Federal do Brasil,[24] the country has approximately 28 million individual income taxpayers, a figure that is many times more than the number of investors in government bonds and equities. Attracting a significant fraction of these taxpayers to invest part of their income in financial products, made available through the equity and debt capital markets, should be front and center in market development initiatives. A higher number of participants will increase liquidity in the primary and secondary markets and ultimately make those markets more efficient.

The concepts, ideas, challenges, and solutions discussed in this article are neither new nor revolutionary. What, then, prevents stakeholders from tackling the problems and seeking improved results? The federal government and market entities have certainly tried to attract more investors to the capital markets,[25] but their efforts have been short term and of limited reach. The true, long-lasting solutions to the development of capital markets in Brazil will surely come from a concerted effort involving all stakeholders, but preconditions must exist. Some of these are currently in place, especially given the low-interest-rate environment, the declared willingness of regulators to make capital markets more efficient, and the unprecedented ease of knowledge sharing through technology. Stakeholders need to seize the current opportunity and work together to develop equity and debt capital markets in Brazil to their true potential for the benefit of the economy and of society.

---

[23]The foremost example is the annual Semana Nacional de Educação Financeira (National Financial Education Week), organized by the Central Bank of Brazil, CVM, Previc (Pension Fund Regulator), and ANBIMA, among others.

[24]Brazil's internal revenue service.

[25]Tax incentives for investors purchasing dêbentures de infraestrutura (infrastructure bonds) and the creation of the Novo Mercado de Renda Fixa (Fixed-Income New Market) by ANBIMA are good examples.

References

Abrapp. 2017. *Consolidado Estatístico*. Associação Brasileira das Entidades Fechadas de Previdência Complementar (August). www.abrapp.org.br/Paginas/consolidadoestatistico.aspx.

ANBIMA. 2017. *Boletim de Mercado de Capitais* (November). www.anbima.com.br/.

Arner, Douglas W., Jànos Barberis, and Ross P. Buckley. 2017. *FinTech and RegTech in a Nutshell, and the Future in a Sandbox*. Charlottesville, VA: CFA Institute Research Foundation.

B3. 2017. "*Perfil de Investidores*" (November). http://www.bmfbovespa.com.br.

Bonomo, Marco. ed. 2004. *Finanças Aplicadas ao Brasil*. 2nd ed. Rio de Janeiro: FGV Editora.

Costa, Roberto T. 2006. *Mercado de Capitais: Uma Trajetória de 50 Anos*. São Paulo, Brazil: Imprensa Oficial do Estado de São Paulo.

Matos, Pedro. 2017. *An Assessment of Dual-Class Shares in Brazil: Evidence from the Novo Mercado Reform*. Charlottesville, VA: CFA Institute; www.cfapubs.org/doi/pdf/10.2469/ccb.v2017.n3.1.

Mendonça de Barros, José Roberto. 2000. *Desafios e Oportunidades para o Mercado de Capitais Brasileiro*. São Paulo, Brazil: Bolsa de Valores de São Paulo.

Miranda, Mauro M. 2017. "Monstros da Nossa Própria Criação: Tecnicidade Excessiva Como Custo de Transação No Mercado de Crédito Privado No Brasil." In *Sistema Financeiro Nacional: O Que Fazer?* ed. Dodl, Alessandra B., and Roberto L. Troster. São Paulo, Brazil: Elsevier.

Simão, Jorge M. 2007. *Debêntures Conversíveis No Brasil: Modelos de Avaliação e Estudos de Casos Reais*. São Paulo, Brazil: Editora Atlas.

Nacional, Tesouro. 2017. *Balanço do Tesouro Direto* (November). www.tesouro.gov.br.

World Federation of Exchanges. 2017. *Monthly Report* (December). www.world-exchanges.org.

3. The Chilean Fixed-Income Market: Evolution and Challenges

Nicolás Álvarez, CFA

This article describes the main characteristics and recent developments of the Chilean fixed-income market. The first section describes the market size, the main types of bonds, and some recent market changes. The second section analyzes the investor base during this period, particularly regarding the sovereign bond segment, and discusses the role of pension funds and nonresident investors. The third section presents quantitative evidence about the degree of the local fixed-income market's international integration. The fourth section summarizes recent regulatory changes that are relevant for the market. The fifth section concludes, with thoughts about challenges remaining for better market development.

TYPES OF BONDS AND MARKET SIZE

Two types of issuers dominate the Chilean fixed-income market: sovereign issuers, which include bonds issued by the Central Bank of Chile and the General Treasury of Chile, and private issuers, which include mainly bank bonds and debentures from nonfinancial or industrial corporations. As of December 2008, the outstanding amount of bonds was USD 67 billion—50% in private sector bonds and 30% in sovereign bonds. Two-thirds of these bonds were denominated in *unidades de fomento* (UF), a monetary unit linked to the Chile Consumer Price Index; the remainder were denominated in Chilean pesos. A bond denominated in UF is inflation protected, like a US TIPS bond.

Since 2008, the outstanding amount increased to USD 143 billion. The composition also changed because of the large amount of bonds issued by the treasury and the banks. The treasury issued a great amount of debt during this period to finance the fiscal deficit. The composition by currency is now more balanced, as shown in **Figure 3.1**: Bonds denominated in UF and Chilean pesos represent 60% and 40%, respectively.

The Chilean fixed-income market is relatively small compared with those of developed economies. As **Figure 3.2** illustrates, Chile's ratio of outstanding bond to GDP is less than 80%, which is lower than the median for OECD countries (129%) but in line with the median of emerging economies (80%).

FIGURE 3.1. TYPES OF DOMESTIC CHILEAN BONDS

A. Outstanding Amount of Chilean Bonds

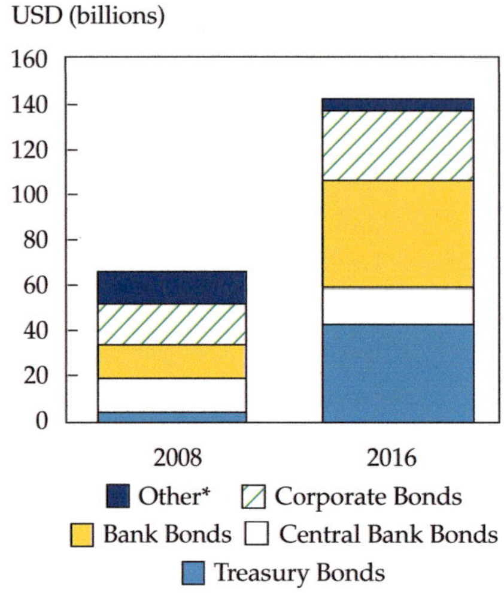

B. Outstanding Share of Chilean Bonds

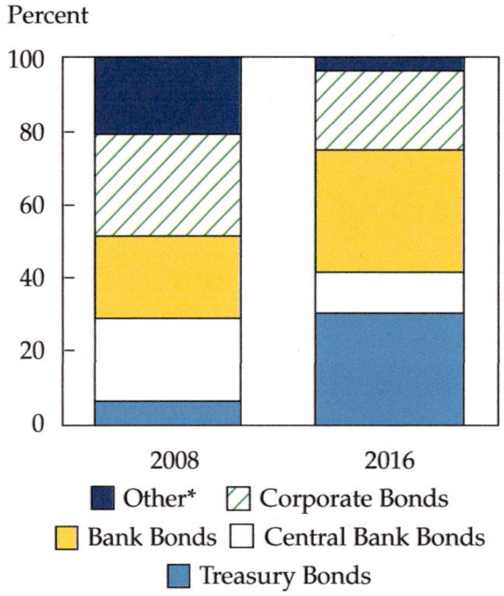

*"Other" includes bank mortgages and securitized bonds.

Source: DCV.

FIGURE 3.2. CHILE'S FIXED-INCOME MARKET DEPTH, 2016

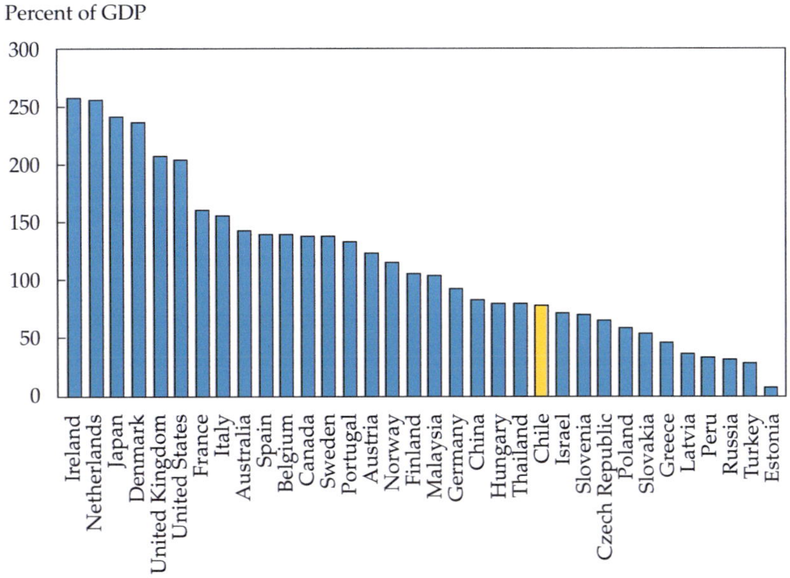

Note: Debt securities = Total debt securities outstanding by residence of issuer.

Sources: Bank for International Settlements (BIS) debt securities statistics database, the Central Bank of Chile, and the Ministry of Finance of Chile.

MAIN PLAYERS IN THE MARKET

The largest investors in the market are pension funds. They manage assets equivalent to 70% of Chilean GDP, with nearly 60% of their portfolios invested in domestic assets and more than 50% in local fixed-income instruments. Therefore, they have a huge influence on the trading and prices of domestic bonds. During the last decade, the importance of pension funds has increased notably: Their holdings increased from USD 30 billion in 2008 to more than USD 70 billion in 2016, mostly in sovereign bonds.

The second-largest investors are life insurance companies, which held USD 24 billion in bonds as of 2016. Compared with pension funds, life insurance companies invest in bonds that have longer maturities, bear larger spreads, and are denominated in UF to match the cash flows of their liabilities, mainly annuities.

Another important development in the market is the greater participation of mutual funds during recent years. Given the lower-interest-rate environment in this period, fixed-income funds have had great performance. Consequently, they have received a significant amount of inflows, which have been invested mainly in bank bonds. This exposure can be expected to change significantly if there is a reversal (rise) in medium- and long-term rates because of the end of liquidity stimulus programs worldwide.

Finally, for liquidity reasons, banks invest mainly in sovereign securities—particularly central bank bonds and/or securities that are accepted by the central bank in repo and similar operations—to get access to short-term liquidity, as shown in **Figure 3.3**.

In particular, exposure to sovereign bonds has changed by holder over recent years. Since 2010, pension funds increased their holdings significantly, moving from 35% to nearly 70% of the outstanding amount in 2016. In the same period, banks reduced their holdings from 30% to 15%. This development could have had a negative impact on the market liquidity of those bonds because pension funds tend to hold those instruments in their portfolios longer than banks do.[26]

This last pattern is also seen across the yield curve. Pension funds hold most of the sovereign bonds with maturities greater than five years. In contrast, banks have concentrated their exposure in bonds with maturities of less than five years—especially in bonds issued by the central bank.

Life insurance companies have almost eliminated their exposure to sovereign bonds, given the lower rates of these bonds, and have replaced them with BBB rated foreign bonds and real estate investments—asset classes with a higher yield and more risk. **Figure 3.4** shows the distribution of domestic sovereign bonds.

Nonresidents, in contrast, invest almost exclusively in sovereign bonds, given their higher liquidity compared with private sector bonds. The preferred sovereign bonds are those denominated in Chilean pesos and issued by the treasury. Nonresidents' holdings have moved in a range between 2% and 8% of the stock of outstanding sovereign bonds. They reached a peak in April 2013 at the same time as the launch of Global Depositary Notes, instruments that facilitate the investment in domestic sovereign. However, after the "taper tantrum" event in the second half of 2013, shown in Panel A of **Figure 3.5**, exposure to fixed income in emerging markets, including Chile, was reduced significantly.

Panel B of Figure 3.5 illustrates that the exposure of nonresident investors to Chilean sovereign bonds is low in both absolute and relative terms. This could have several explanations, including operational and tax barriers, issues that have been partially resolved

[26]See Central Bank of Chile (2017) for more details on this issue.

FIGURE 3.3. MAIN PLAYERS IN THE CHILEAN FIXED-INCOME MARKET

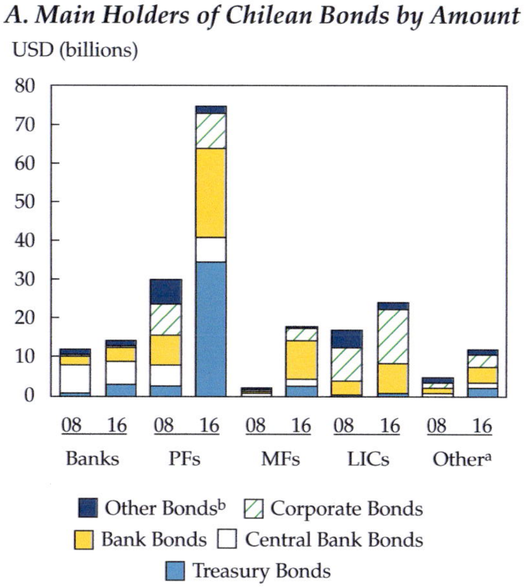

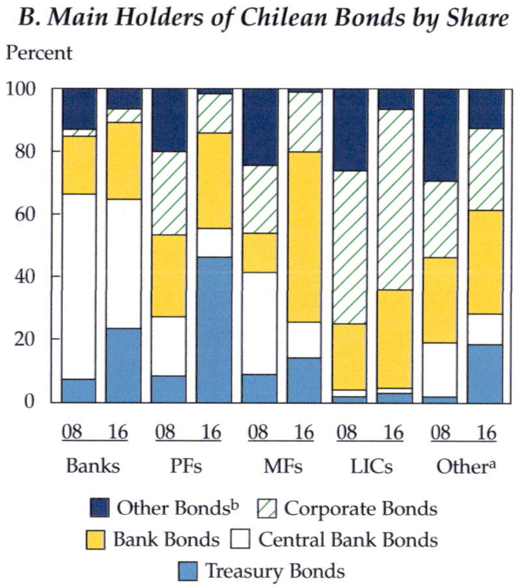

[a]"Other" includes mainly broker/dealers, closed-end funds, and nonresidents.

[b]"Other bonds" includes bank mortgages and securitized bonds.

Notes: LICs are life insurance companies; MFs are mutual funds; and PFs are pension funds.

Source: DCV.

FIGURE 3.4. INVESTORS IN THE SOVEREIGN BOND MARKET

A. Share in Domestic Sovereign Bonds

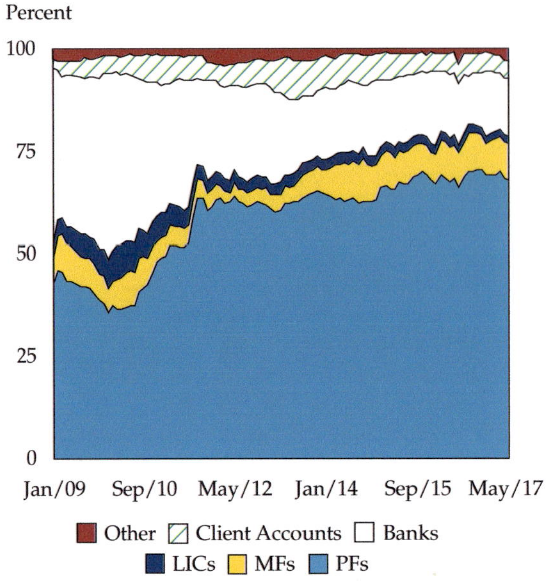

B. Share in Domestic Sovereign Bonds by Maturity

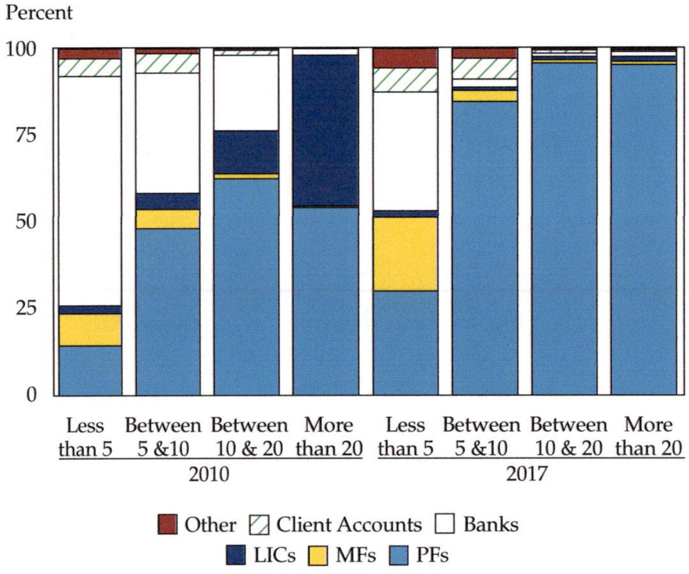

Notes: LICs are life insurance companies; MFs are mutual funds; and PFs are pension funds.

Source: DCV.

FIGURE 3.5. SHARE OF NONRESIDENT INVESTORS IN DOMESTIC SOVEREIGN BONDS

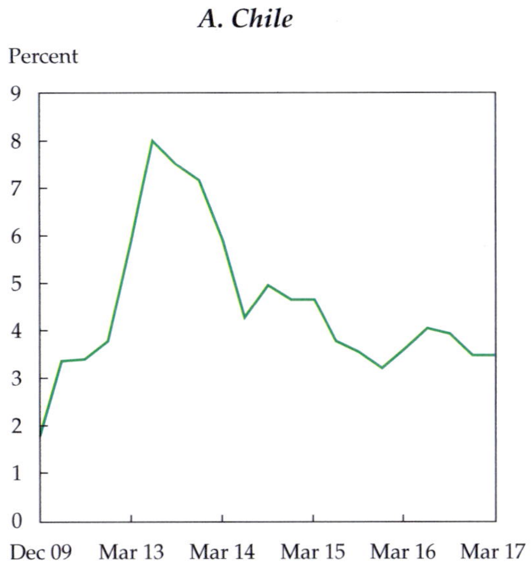

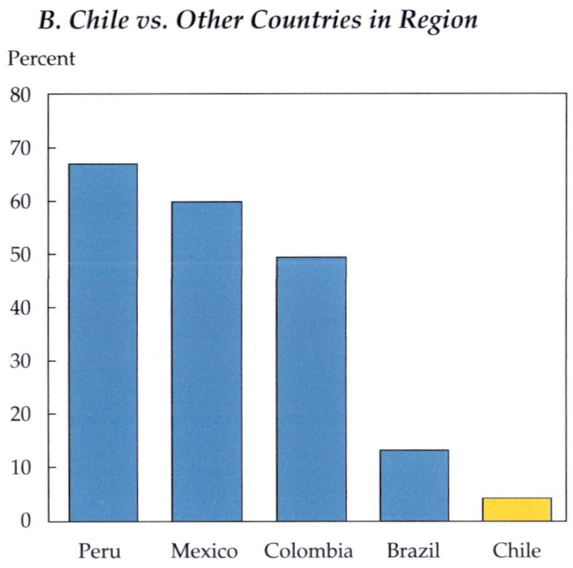

Note: Panel B data are as of 2015.

Sources: Central Bank of Chile, central banks of individual countries, and the IMF.

recently (see the fourth section of this article); likely the most important reason is the lack of market size or market depth. Those issues, in addition to the large presence of pension funds, make it difficult for nonresidents to access the sovereign bond market.

INTEGRATION WITH INTERNATIONAL MARKETS

Integration of the Chilean fixed-income market with international markets can be measured by analyzing price co-movements. Such integration seems to be relatively moderate. The "taper tantrum" that occurred between April and September 2013 made that clear, as **Figure 3.6** shows. During this period, when most countries' rates rose substantially, Chilean sovereign long-term rates moved hardly at all.

FIGURE 3.6. LONG-TERM SOVEREIGN RATES DURING THE "TAPER TANTRUM" EVENT

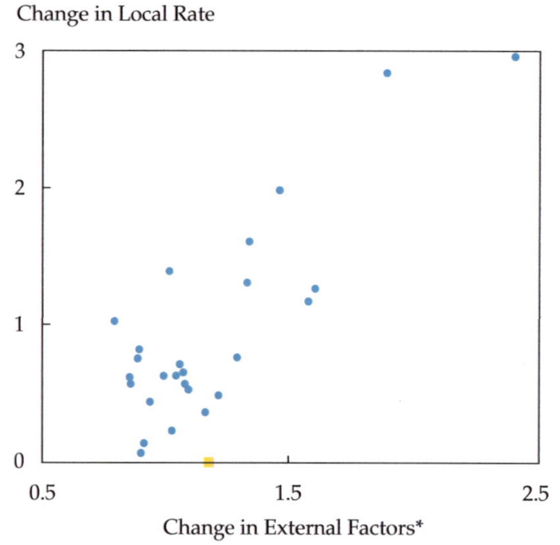

Note: Change between 30 April and 30 September 2013. Includes Australia, Belgium, Brazil, Chile (in yellow), China, Colombia, South Korea, Slovakia, Philippines, Finland, France, Netherlands, Indonesia, Israel, Italy, Japan, Malaysia, Mexico, New Zealand, Norway, Peru, United Kingdom, Czech Republic, Russia, South Africa, Sweden, Switzerland, Thailand, and Turkey.

*Ten-year US Treasury bond rate plus the five-year CDS rate.

Sources: Central Bank of Chile and Bloomberg.

To analyze this finding more deeply, this article uses an approach based on uncovered interest rate parity as follows:

$$i_t = i_t^* + E_t\left(\Delta S_{t+T}\right) + \rho_t,$$

where i_t is the domestic interest rate, i_t^* is the relevant foreign interest rate, $E_t\left(\Delta S_{t+T}\right)$ is expected exchange rate depreciation, and ρ_t is a risk premium factor that controls for default, government leverage, market liquidity, political risk, and so forth.

Applying an OLS model, the main findings, as shown in **Table 3.1**, are the following:

1. The pass-through coefficient from the external rate to the local rate is between 0.13 and 0.59, depending on the local rate used (real or nominal, cash or derivatives market). In other words, if external rates increase by 100 bps, local rates could increase, on average, by between 13 and 59 bps.

2. For the cash (bond) market, domestic institutional investors—basically, pension funds—have a significant influence on rates.

The pass-through coefficient from the external rate to the local rate is lower in Chile than in other emerging markets. The median coefficient is 0.5, much lower than in other Latin American countries, such as Colombia (1.5), Mexico (1.4), Brazil (1.35), and Peru (1.1); in all these markets, nonresident investors have great influence on the bond sovereign market, as shown in **Figure 3.7**.

MAIN REGULATORY CHANGES AND OTHER DEVELOPMENTS

Recently, several legal and regulatory changes have occurred that affect Chile's fixed-income market, with particular relevance for nonresident investors. In general, foreign investors face several barriers when they decide to invest in fixed income in Chile:

- the duty to report to the Servicio de Impuestos Internos (SII, the Chilean equivalent of the US Internal Revenue Service) and the Central Bank of Chile

- tax regulations

- current market conditions

TABLE 3.1. DETERMINANTS OF THE 10-YEAR CHILEAN SOVEREIGN RATES (*P*-VALUES IN PARENTHESES)

	Nominal 10	Swap Nom. 10	UF 10	Swap UF 10
	0.334***	0.585***	0.131**	0.369***
	(0.000)	(0.000)	(0.016)	(0.000)
	0.015	0.028	−0.266***	−0.205
	(0.220)	(0.104)	(0.005)	(0.119)
	0.460***	0.458***	0.192***	−0.175**
	(0.000)	(0.003)	(0.009)	(0.033)
*tpm**	0.801***	0.770***	0.054	−0.009
	(0.000)	(0.005)	(0.614)	(0.970)
g^e	0.396***	0.458***	0.431***	0.550***
	(0.000)	(0.000)	(0.000)	(0.000)
Inst. inv.	−0.023***	0.005	−0.020***	0.009
	(0.000)	(0.253)	(0.000)	(0.107)
constant	3.438***	0.775	1.379**	−0.621
	(0.000)	(0.333)	(0.033)	(0.258)
N	129	128	134	128
R^2	0.74	0.72	0.64	0.75
R^2 adjusted	0.72	0.71	0.62	0.74

Notes: Monthly data from January 2014 to March 2015. See **Appendix A** for variables' definitions. "Nominal" and "UF" rates refer to the cash market (bonds), and "Swap" refers to the derivatives market.

*Statistically significant at 10% level.

**Statistically significant at 5% level.

***Statistically significant at 1% level.

FIGURE 3.7. PASS-THROUGH COEFFICIENT FROM EXTERNAL TO LOCAL 10-YEAR RATES BY MARKET

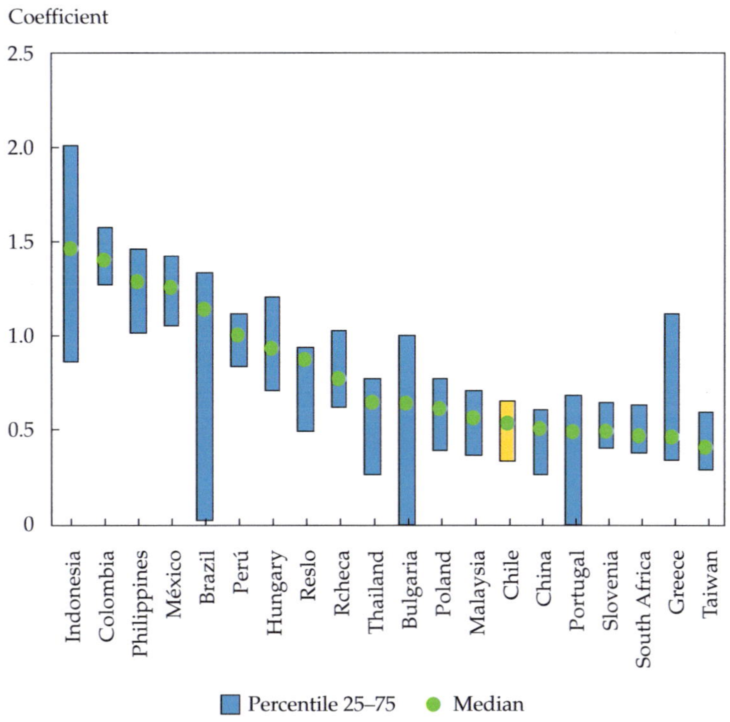

Notes: Specification similar to the OLS model seen in Table 3.1. Coefficients reported are those associated with the T-bond rate. A rolling OLS model, with windows of 36 months, was estimated from 2005 to 2015.

The SII requires that nonresident investors request an RUT (Rol Único Tributario) number—that is, a tax ID—to declare their taxes. Between 2000 and 2011, the SII eased this requirement; international securities depositories (such as Euroclear Bank) or other local financial agents may request foreign exchange transactions on behalf of foreign investors under their own RUT. In 2017, reporting duties required by the Central Bank of Chile also were similarly eased.

The main tax requirements for fixed-income securities are stated in Article 104 of the Chilean income tax law. This article was modified in 2014 by the Ley Única de Fondos (LUF), which provides a capital gains tax exemption for the entire stock of sovereign bonds. Previously, only a subset of sovereign bonds had this benefit. In 2016, withholding tax[27] conditions and trading requirements to qualify for the capital gains tax exemption were also eased. For example, bonds purchased over the counter now qualify for this benefit. Previously, all transactions had to be on stock exchanges.

Given recent regulatory changes, Euroclear Bank started to operate in Chile, making transactions and custody of bonds easier for foreign investors.

FUTURE CHALLENGES

The Chilean fixed-income market has thrived since the financial crisis. Today, the market is deeper—its depth is similar to that of fixed-income markets in other emerging economies. The market is also more attractive for local and foreign investors because of several changes in Chile's income tax law. These are among the factors Euroclear probably considered when opening its business in Chile. For these and other reasons, the Chilean fixed-income market is getting more attention from international benchmark providers, such as JPMorgan and Standard & Poor's.

Chile is facing some challenges in the near term. Pension funds dominate the market, which is good with regard to the supply of funds but less promising from the perspective of market liquidity and integration with international markets. As shown earlier in this article, co-movements between local and foreign long-term rates have been low, in part because of the large influence of pension funds on the market.

Because of this influence, especially in the sovereign bond market, nonresident investors continue to find it challenging to get access. The volume in the secondary market is low, so foreign investors can only get Chilean sovereign bond exposure mainly through primary auctions.

Pension funds are now getting more flexibility regarding the asset classes in which they can invest. In 2017, private equity, real estate, and infrastructure bonds were allowed by the regulator as new asset classes and probably will soon be part of their portfolios. This will be a favorable development for the local fixed-income market because it could provide an opportunity for other investors—for example, nonresidents—to increase their fixed-income exposure.

[27]Currently at 4%.

APPENDIX A. VARIABLES IN THE OLS MODEL

1. i_t^* = External rate (i_t^*) = US 10-year Treasury rate, nominal or real
2. $E_t(\Delta S_{t+T})$ = Expected change in the FX spot rate at two years
3. EMBI Chile
4. tpm^* = Surprise in domestic monetary policy rate
5. g^e = Economic growth expectation at one year
6. Inst. Inv. = Share of PFs and MFs in the sovereign bond market, lagged in one month

References

Álvarez, Nicolás, and Luis Gonzales. 2016. "Determinantes de Tasas de Largo Plazo en Chile". Mimeo.

Central Bank of Chile. 2013. "Financial Stability Report Second Half 2013." www.bcentral.cl/web/central-bank-of-chile/-/financial-stability-report-second-half-2-16.

Central Bank of Chile. 2015. "Financial Stability Report Second Half 2015." www.bcentral.cl/web/central-bank-of-chile/-/financial-stability-report-second-half-2--1.

Central Bank of Chile. 2017. "Financial Stability Report First Half 2017." www.bcentral.cl/web/central-bank-of-chile/-/financial-stability-report-first-half-2017.

4. Colombia: Avid Investors Clash with a Narrow Set of Investment Opportunities

César Cuervo, CFA

INTRODUCTION

Capital markets in Colombia are more developed and liquid than many participants in the global investor community think. Nevertheless, significant opportunities for growth in all asset classes and for a greater role for capital markets in general exist. In other words, ample room for improvement in achieving the macro goal of the markets is available, which would make capital allocation more efficient and boost economic growth and prosperity.

This article is by no means a comprehensive assessment of all capital markets in Colombia, but rather an attempt to diagnose and analyze a series of issues that, if improved, should contribute to making those markets more functional. As will be shown, the evolution of securities markets in Colombia requires the involvement of many parties, including those in the real economy and not just those in the financial sector.

EQUITY: INVESTORS DEMAND MORE ALTERNATIVES

The local equity market is clearly underdeveloped. The ratio of total market capitalization to nominal GDP as of December 2016 was 37%, in line with the average emerging market but far below the world figure of 97%.[28] In fact, Colombia's ratio has fallen consistently over the last five years, coming down from 70% in 2012.

In addition, Colombia's equity market is not a good proxy for the economy in terms of industry exposure. Even though economic sector weights have varied dramatically over the last decade, that inconsistency between equity markets and the real economy has persisted. In 2010–2011, with energy prices rallying in the aftermath of the

[28]Measured as the world's total market capitalization divided by the world's total GDP.

Great Recession, oil and gas names represented over 30% of the COLCAP (Colombian Capitalization Equity) Index, even though the hydrocarbons sector never topped 15% in the real economy. Today, the construction and infrastructure sector represents approximately 8% of GDP but has a weight of less than 0.5% in the equity index.

This divergence forces investors seeking exposure to the underlying fundamentals of the economy to look for alternatives in private markets. For example, the inability to find liquid names in infrastructure or real estate has helped develop alternative asset classes. However, the lack of investment opportunities in economic sectors available in traditional asset classes is an obstacle for attracting investors, especially from abroad, to public equity. Successful regional initiatives, such as the creation of the Pacific Alliance bloc, are sensible ways to bypass this issue and obtain the diversification benefits of investing regionally. Still, investors would greatly appreciate a better selection of economic sectors within the Colombian public market.

Liquidity is a concern. Colombian equities are far less liquid than those of other Latin American countries. Total trading volume has decreased sharply since its peak in 2012 and is currently a mere COP 169 billion (~USD 57 million) per day, above Peru and Argentina but significantly below Chile, Mexico, and, of course, Brazil. Also, only 10–15 names consistently trade more than USD 1 million per day.

The depreciation of the Colombian peso has certainly played a role in the contraction of trading volumes; the exchange rate has gone up from less than COP 1,800 per US dollar in mid-2012 to COP 3,000 per US dollar today. However, even when measured in local currency terms, daily trading volumes have fallen by about 35% over that same period. Hence, the decline must be due to factors other than exchange rates.

Market performance has not helped either. The average yearly return of 5.2% (plus dividends) in the 2007–16 period and the 3.3% (plus dividends) compound annual return for the 10-year period ending in September 2017 are not particularly attractive. However, this was not unique among emerging markets, and the high volatility of the last decade was rewarding to investors who timed the cycle.

The increasingly limited set of listed companies seems to be the clue to the decline in trading. Despite several IPOs between 2007 and 2012, equity capital market activity and M&A (as well as several bankruptcies) over the last decade have shrunk the number of equity issuers from 98 in 2004 (already a very small number for a country of Colombia's size) to 69 in 2017.[29] Accordingly, investors have a very thin base of names to choose from, correlations increase, and the benefits of diversification within Colombia dwindle.

[29]World Federation of Exchanges (2017), www.world-exchanges.org/home/index.php/statistics.

For a country with a population of almost 50 million[30] and a total GDP of USD 283 billion,[31] 69 issuers is a very low number by any standard. The problem, however, is not a lack of potential issuers. By the end of 2016, excluding financials, Colombia had 37 companies with more than USD 1 billion per year in operating revenue and 130 with more than USD 300 million. Furthermore, at least 80 out of the 1,000 largest companies had a book value of over USD 300 million, while almost 200 had book values of USD 100 million[32] or more. Including the financial sector—banks, insurance companies, and asset managers and trusts—would make these figures considerably higher.

Figure 4.1 shows the decline in the number of Colombian listed companies, as well as their fluctuating market capitalization, for 2005–2017. **Figure 4.2** shows the price appreciation and trading volume of the COLCAP Index of Colombian equities for 2005–2017.

FIGURE 4.1. COLOMBIAN LISTED COMPANIES AND MARKET CAPITALIZATION, 2005–2017

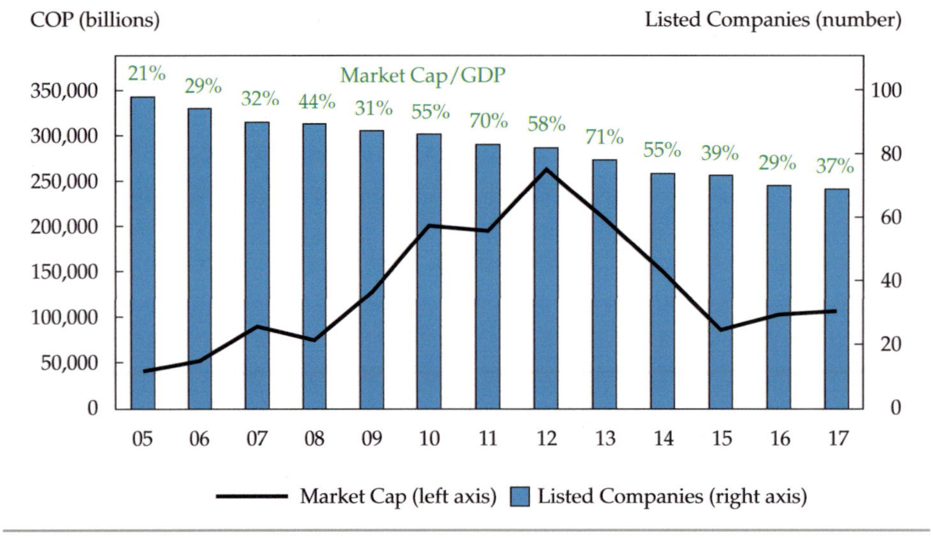

Source: World Federation of Exchanges.

[30]49.6 million as of December 2017; Departamento Nacional de Estadística (DANE), www.dane.gov.co/reloj/.

[31]Data from the Departamento Nacional de Estadística (DANE); GDP at current prices.

[32]Publicaciones Semana, Colombia Revista Semana, Edición Especial: Las 100 empresas más grandes de Colombia (29 April 2017).

FIGURE 4.2. COLOMBIAN CAPITALIZATION INDEX AND TRADED VOLUME, 2005–2017

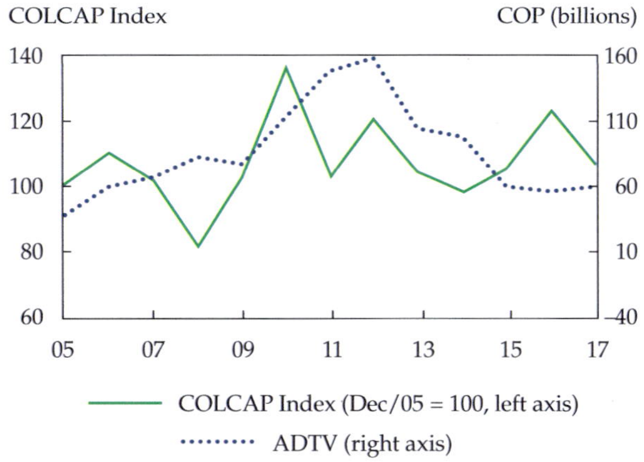

Note: "ADTV" is average daily traded volume.

Sources: World Federation of Exchanges and Bloomberg.

Through its flagship Colombia Capital program, the Colombia Stock Exchange (BVC) has been working hard to bring more issuers to the market. The number of member companies keeps growing because the program has been successful in explaining the benefits of accessing capital markets to management teams and shareholders. Although the BVC has managed to increase the number of corporate debt issuers, results have been much more modest in the equity space.

Colombia has a big base of potential equity issuers. The BVC has led a continuous institutional effort to convince more companies to list their stock, and the investor community is consistently asking for more investment choices. Hence, the reasons the equity market remains so undeveloped lie elsewhere. Possible reasons for this lack of development that are not directly related to the capital markets are discussed later in this article.

A closer look at the data reveals that over the past 10 years, total market capitalization has not fallen in the same proportion as trading volumes. In fact, it has grown significantly, from around USD 50 billion in early 2007 to almost USD 120 billion as of September 2017. Granted, part of this growth has been explained by the state-controlled integrated oil company Ecopetrol listing its shares in late 2007, with roughly USD 20.5 billion of market cap today. However, a simple cross-sectional comparison within Latin America shows that the Colombian exchange is not particularly accessible to small caps. The average Colombian company has a market cap of USD 1.6 billion, compared with less than USD 1 billion for Chile and Argentina and no more than USD 400 million for Peru. Colombia is lagging in developing its small-cap segment, which, in turn, affects the development of other asset classes—namely, private equity.

Since the mid-2000s, financial regulation has made it possible to use alternatives, especially private equity funds, as suitable investments for private pension plans, and the maximum allocation authorized has increased gradually, as has actual investment in this asset class. As of September 2017, the total amount invested in private equity (at current holding value) by the moderate (Moderado) fund is USD 4.1 billion, or 6.6% of the fund's assets under management. About 75% of this private equity total is invested in international private equity funds. The local private equity industry, representing the remaining 25%, has also benefited from regulatory changes that enabled Colombian general partners to develop that sector. As conceived by the local financial regulator, the private equity fund structure can support different types of private investments, including infrastructure and real estate. However, several buyout and venture capital funds have also raised capital and currently hold positions in a wide variety of companies, different sizes, and sectors: 20-plus different Colombian GPs with nearly 50 investment strategies. Unfortunately, these funds struggle to find efficient exit plans. With no relevant market for IPOs of small caps, they are almost forced to cash out via private M&A.

Local institutional investors in Colombia are not particularly fond of smaller companies. Given the size of pension funds, for instance, it may be relatively inefficient to allocate valuable resources to analyzing smaller and less liquid names, which are unlikely to represent a large enough exposure in an overall portfolio to make a difference. This shortcoming feeds a vicious cycle in which smaller institutions and retail investors also tend to avoid smaller names because of poor market sentiment or the expectation that investment inflows from large players will not occur.

Promoting the small-cap sector, then, should benefit both the public and private equity markets. Facilitating the use of public markets as exit strategies for private equity funds should bolster IPOs of mid-size and small-cap companies. Further, encouraging investment in small caps by institutional investors, such as private pension plans (probably not through the largest moderate multifund but through the smaller, higher-risk ones and through voluntary retirement plans) and mutual funds, will be key for developing the segment. Finally, tax benefits for smaller companies that list their equity could incentivize management teams of privately held entities to approach the market. Local regulation has gone through an exceptional transformation to foster private equity; "completing the cycle" by endorsing public small caps seems like the natural next step.

FIXED INCOME: MUCH BETTER BUT STILL ROOM FOR IMPROVEMENT

In terms of development and liquidity, the fixed-income and FX markets are completely different stories. Regarding the latter, the spot market is liquid enough, with average daily volume of over USD 950 million in 2017.

In the sovereign and corporate debt markets managed by the BVC, trading volume exceeds COP 4.3 trillion per day (~USD 1.4 billion)[33] in total. In addition, the central bank has another fixed-income platform exclusively for sovereign debt in local currency (which works with a highly functional market-makers program) with a daily volume of roughly another USD 1 billion.[34] The Ministry of Finance has relied on frequent and consistent access to global and local bond markets for decades, regardless of presidential changes and political swings. Accordingly, the national government has prudently developed and maintained the sovereign debt markets, as shown in **Figure 4.3**: COP fixed rate, inflation linked, and USD denominated. A deep and liquid market for government debt is the result of this long-lasting effort.

The corporate credit market, as shown in **Figure 4.4**, is less robust. In almost any jurisdiction in emerging markets, institutional investors—particularly, life insurance companies and pension funds—are natural buyers of corporate credit. However, in smaller markets like Colombia, it is more difficult to develop the corporate bond market because long-term investors tend to absorb new issues, virtually eliminating liquidity.

Bonds denominated in hard currency tend to be more liquid: They are targeted to a wider investor community, trade on global transactional platforms, allow investors to buy credit risk without facing exchange rate risk (at least not directly), and are typically issued by relatively large corporations. In the case of Colombia, the latter include only a few names, such as the large financial institutions, Ecopetrol, and six or seven other corporate issuers. In fact, only 31 different issues and 15 separate Colombian issuers are included in the CEMBI Latam Index.[35]

However, corporate debt instruments denominated in Colombian pesos, especially those of longer maturity, are far less liquid than bonds denominated in hard currencies, even though the number of issuers has grown steadily over the last 10 years. Institutional investors seek to buy these securities, very often in the primary market, and hold the positions until maturity because they seek to match these assets against

[33]2017 year-to-date averages as of 30 September 2017. Figures include repos and securities lending for equities and fixed income and primary market transactions for fixed income.

[34]Bonds' face value; 2017 year-to-date averages as of 30 September 2017.

[35]JPMorgan Corporate Emerging Markets Bond Index Latin America as of 30 September 2017.

FIGURE 4.3. SOVEREIGN DEBT: TESCOP (FIXED-RATE) AUCTIONS PER MATURITY

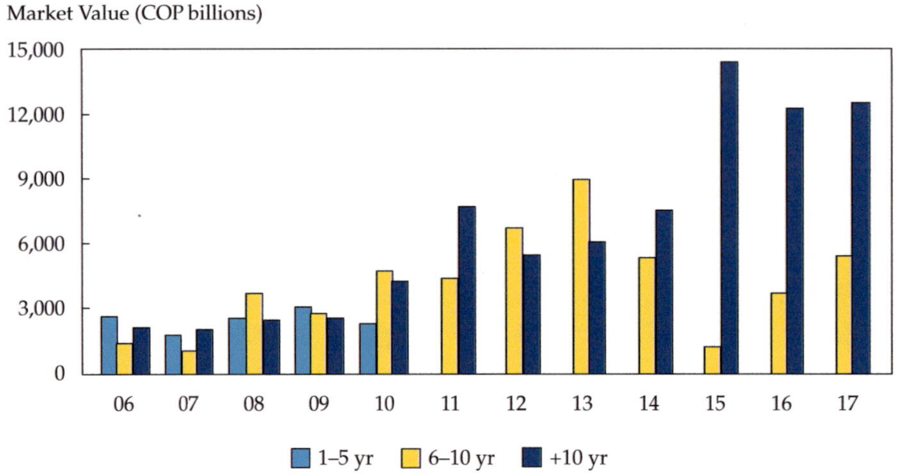

Source: Banco de la República.

FIGURE 4.4. CORPORATE DEBT: PRIMARY OFFERINGS, 2007–2016

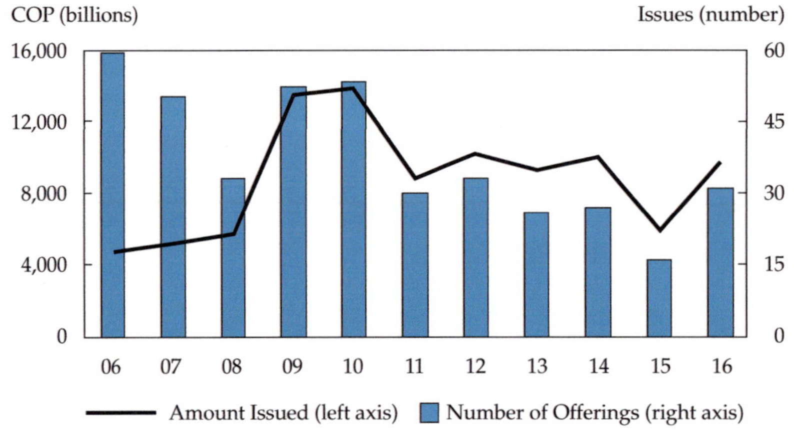

Source: BVC.

their long-term, peso-denominated liabilities. Even though this is not a problem for issuers with regard to their capital structure and financial needs, it translates into almost no liquidity for local corporate debt. It might thus prove difficult to establish a market-maker program for such debt. Yet, creating issuance structures to include tranches designed to provide liquidity and price discovery for all bonds in the credit rating versus maturity grid could boost market depth and liquidity.

Regulation of pension funds also hampers the development of this market. The risk control model adopted by the Colombian regulator for the pension fund system and the insurance industry is stringent. Over the last decade, the Financial Superintendence of Colombia (SFC) has provided flexibility and successfully kept up with change in financial technology, allowing and properly regulating new instruments and entire asset classes. But investors still eagerly await some regulatory changes, either in the form of additional authorized suitable investments or bigger regulatory "buckets" in the investment regime for certain segments.

In an attempt to control credit risk and protect pension fund members from unrecoverable losses, local regulations prior to the last modification in May 2016 forbade private pension fund managers from investing in high-yield debt, either international or local. Hence, they could not purchase any issuance with a local credit rating below BBB–. Also, the face value of debt holdings in the portfolio had to be written down once two major rating agencies downgraded the issuer below investment grade. This restriction seriously hindered the growth and development of the corporate bond market.

In practice, unless an issuer knows that the new bond will be rated BBB– or higher (local rating), the issuance will simply not take place. Since the changes in 2016, natural buyers may invest in high-yield bonds, but regulatory risk perception is still high and the maximum allocation is still small (1% for the moderate fund and 4% for the higher-risk fund). Also, the bucket must be shared with other assets under the label of "restricted investments."

This limitation has severe second-round effects for capital markets in Colombia, with negative consequences beyond corporate debt. Most companies use debt issuance in local currency as their first approach to public capital markets; hard-currency debt and equity will be lower priorities regarding the capital structure. At the same time, it is difficult for the average mid-size Colombian company to exhibit financial indicators sufficiently robust to secure an investment-grade rating, even in local credit rating scales, which keeps corporate Colombia from dropping traditional (and often more expensive) bank lending and accessing debt markets, let alone seeking fresh equity to finance growth. Creating a high-yield market in Colombia would not only enhance risk-budgeting tools for portfolio managers but also facilitate access to capital markets for Colombian companies.

ESG AND LESSONS LEARNED FROM IPO HISTORY

THE RIGHTS OF MINORITY SHAREHOLDERS

Environmental, social, and governance (ESG) considerations deserve a whole article about their impact on the development of capital markets in Colombia, particularly when related to governance issues in the equity space. Although the list of opportunities for improvement may be quite long, three governance issues need to be addressed for equity markets to develop and (re)gain investor confidence: (1) the treatment of minority shareholders, (2) the pricing of IPOs, and (3) the recurrent use of nonvoting shares.

Looking at the recent history of the Colombian market shown in **Figure 4.5**, it is not surprising that the highest number of offerings—both primary and follow-ons—coincided with the market peak between late 2010 and 2012. The Colombian market has not had an IPO since the Cemex Latam Holdings IPO in November 2012. In the 2013–17 period, equity capital markets activity consisted of follow-on offerings, public offers of equity holdings owned by state-controlled entities, and tender offers, as **Figure 4.6** shows. The latter have reduced the number of companies listed, decreasing even further investors' portfolio diversification options.

FIGURE 4.5. COLOMBIA EQUITY OFFERINGS VS. MARKET PERFORMANCE AND VALUATION, 2008–2016

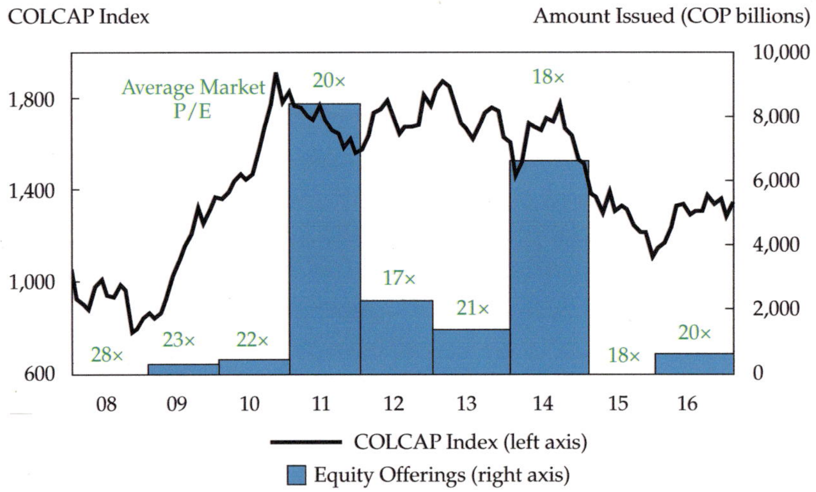

Sources: BVC and Bloomberg.

FIGURE 4.6. COLOMBIA EQUITY OFFERINGS, 2007–2016

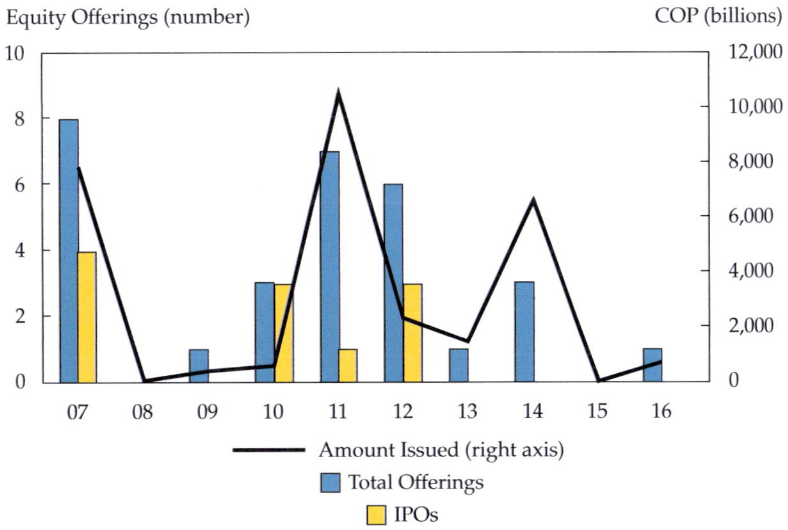

Source: BVC.

The market downturn and large decline of Colombian equity price/earnings multiples in the 2013–15 period explain much of the drought in equity capital market activity. However, according to many investors, the poor relative performance of IPOs versus the market aggregate is also to blame for IPOs coming to a full stop.

The evidence seems compelling. With only one noticeable exception, the IPOs that took place between 2010 and 2012, when the market was peaking, have posted lackluster relative returns as of September 2017: Four out of six IPOs have underperformed the COLCAP Index, while one had a mediocre five-year cumulative outperformance of 10%. Only 6 out of 14 liquid offerings (including primary and follow-on) issued in 2010–2012 had positive performance in absolute terms in the five years following the issuance.

In some cases, the seemingly desperate liquidity needs of previous shareowners led some of these investors to dump part of their shares right after the lockup period ended (sometimes, the IPO did not even include a lockup period clause), with the stock eventually selling below the initial IPO price. This has led many investors to lose confidence in the structuring, underwriting, and pricing processes followed in bringing new names to the market.

To recover, markets must regain trust. The first issue to address should be the prospectus of the offering, especially those clauses designed to protect the rights of smaller investors (e.g., lockup period, declaration of controlling shareholder, and treatment of minority shareholders in case of major strategic decisions or corporate restructurings). This article does not aim to enumerate past disappointments, but recent IPO history in Colombia offers some examples for potential issuers, advisers, and regulators.

Pricing, of course, is also a crucial factor. The common practice in Colombia is for an issuer and its advisers to set the price of the offering without book-building. Thus, the investor decision to participate is a dichotomy: The investor either accepts the price set by the issuer or not. Without a book-building process, no price formation is available prior to the issuance and market agents cannot reflect their interest in, and estimates of fundamental value of, the shares.

Forcing all issuers to use book building might work against increasing the number of companies listed. Also, using this process for increases in the book capital of names already listed could be unnecessary because these securities are regularly subject to proper price formation in the secondary market. However, book building is a transparent way to set the price of an IPO and certainly is more aligned with the rights of minority shareholders. Incentives should be in place for issuers to prefer this method, while advisers and company owners should be willing to set prices in a way that allows upside to be shared with new investors.

Structures deserve some commentary as well. With the intention of democratizing free float as much as possible, some IPOs went too far: Some structures allowed very small blocks to be purchased. On top of that, because of the chronic lack of issuers, very high bid-to-cover ratios led to pro rata allocation, which in some extreme cases resulted in blocks of USD 500 to USD 750 for the average investor. These cases proved that having a large number of new shareholders is not necessarily the same as achieving high liquidity: Price formation was not efficient, and shares took longer than expected to gain traction in the secondary market.

It may not be advisable to allocate big blocks exclusively to institutional investors because it also might hinder liquidity. However, investment banks and underwriters should grant access to institutional investors while providing structures that allow democratization. Doing so would maximize participation of all market agents and facilitate regular trade and consolidation of the shareholder base. Some of the few successful experiences Colombia has had in recent years involved different tranches for different types of investors, which shows that this feature should always be considered when structuring new offerings.

Nonvoting shares, referred to as "preferred"[36] by market agents, are also controversial. These securities have gained popularity as an appealing way to raise capital and finance

[36]Different from preferred shares in the United States, which are a "mezzanine" instrument with a fixed dividend payment and a higher claim on the company's assets than common stock.

growth: Controlling shareholders potentially dilute their economic interest in the company (although many issues grant preferential subscription rights) but preserve control of the company. Issuing preferred shares has become mainstream, to the point that several companies will not consider listing common equity. In these cases, the average minority investor has no voting power.

Current regulation dictates that preferred shares must convey to shareholders' economic benefits greater than those of common shares. The former will grant a minimum dividend payment, but in practice, the dividend is equal to that of common shares. Further, at inception, preferred shares can provide an additional economic benefit in the form of a higher dividend payment during a certain period—usually no longer than two or three years. After that period, the economic rights of common and preferred shares are virtually the same,[37] unless otherwise stated in the issue prospectus and/or the company bylaws.

In line with this practice and considering only the value of voting rights, preferred shares should trade at a discount to common shares. For liquidity reasons, this is seldom the case. Sometimes, preferred shares are more liquid than common shares and hence trade at a premium because investors value liquidity more than voting rights. This is most evident when the liquidity differential widens as companies issue American depositary receipts/American depositary shares and make them convertible into preferred shares rather than common ones. The investors' apparent disregard for voting rights provides interesting empirical evidence on the market value of liquidity and is deserving of further research.

Issuing shares with no voting rights is not a flawed practice per se and could benefit the development of capital markets. For companies timidly approaching the market for the first time, preferred stock can be a less invasive way to access capital, avoiding the dilution of control that makes entrepreneurs hesitate to list equity. Adopting best practices from different jurisdictions could help. For example, Chilean Series B shares have less voting power than common equity and virtually no possibility of controlling the company but grant the right to jointly appoint one board member to represent the interests of Series B shareowners.

The use and abuse of preferred shares, however, poses risks for minority shareholders and calls for additional protection of their rights. ESG-driven global investors could become concerned about nonvoting stocks, and index providers might be tempted to exclude preferred shares from the list of names considered for future inclusion in indexes.

[37]Except for the precedence of preferred shares over common shares in case of a liquidation process.

BEYOND MARKET DYNAMICS

Situations not linked to market dynamics have also eroded investor confidence, hampering market development. For example, in an overly publicized episode, one of the largest local broker/dealers was closed by the SFC and liquidated in the fourth quarter of 2012. The firm faced imminent insolvency and several charges of securities fraud, including breach of trust, market manipulation, and misrepresentation. Apart from the obvious effect on public opinion, the collapse of the firm took a toll on trading volume and overall market liquidity.

A series of isolated events more directly related to the governance of issuers also has hurt sentiment regarding local equities. Corruption trials of management members linked to political scandals, the meteoric rise and resounding collapse of a large oil producer, and some violations of minority shareholders' rights have made the headlines in recent years. These cases demonstrate that capital markets in Colombia face difficulties in regard to supervision.

The Financial Superintendence of Colombia has done a remarkable job regulating markets and market agents. Furthermore, the Superintendence has been open and willing to embrace best practices from fellow regulators around the world, seeking a favorable balance between protecting investors and clients of financial institutions on one side and promoting market modernization and development on the other. However, the examples already cited suggest that there is room for improvement regarding prevention practices and controls of market participants, including issuers and financial intermediaries.

Capital markets do not function in isolation, and their current condition in Colombia reflects some of the challenges that the real economy faces. Accordingly, tackling some issues not directly related to capital markets should benefit their development. Formalization is one such issue. Colombia has an informal economy by almost any metric (bank loans to GDP at 45%–50%, employees with social security below 52%, etc.). Although Colombia's highly informal economy is a major opportunity for growth and penetration of products and services, it is also an obstacle to improving the quality of management, increasing governance standards, and accessing capital. Greater formalization should, directly and indirectly, translate into stronger, deeper capital markets.

Widening the base of companies suitable to enter the capital market is a prerequisite for growth in the corporate bonds and equities market. The fiscal reform of 2012 greatly boosted formality in the labor market because companies had more incentives to hire employees under proper conditions—namely, formal contributions to social security (health and pension plans). This, in turn, generated unprecedented growth in contributions to private pension plans, increasing the funds available for efficient capital allocation and investment.

Regulators, financial institutions, and the academic community have long debated a related topic: capping the interest rates banks can charge their clients. Today, interest rates are effectively capped, and it is illegal for any person or entity to lend above that threshold. Although this law seeks to protect the Colombian people from abuses by banking institutions, it has negative effects on the economy and, ultimately, on capital markets.

First, the existence of an interest rate cap leads to informal (shadow) lending outside the financial system. Some agents with no access to formal lending must choose between postponing investment and using their own capital at a higher opportunity cost, facing financial inefficiency either way. However, most individuals and smaller enterprises seeking financing will inevitably search for alternative yet informal (and occasionally illegal) loan providers. Doing so results in higher financial expenses, pressuring the bottom line and profitability.

Second, the existence of maximum interest rates led universal banks to virtually abandon the microcredit segment. Even though niche players have gradually filled this space, it is still severely underpenetrated (microcredit is less than 3% of total loans: 1.3% of GDP), especially considering that Colombia is largely a country made of small- and medium-sized enterprises and the self-employed. Several studies (ANIF 2012, 2015, 2017) show that this underpenetration is a direct consequence of the usury rate framework.

Greater banking penetration and more competition among financial institutions would mean more bond issues for funding and eventually more banks coming to the equity market to raise capital. Colombian lawmakers should closely follow the case of Gentera in Mexico as a clear example of the benefits of a more liberalized, market-driven interest rate framework. Giving more companies access to formal credit leads to higher profitability and, ultimately, to more candidates approaching capital markets as potential issuers of securities.

Finally, two other elements have held back Colombian capital markets. These "legacy" factors, particularly the first, have been difficult to control and have had a remarkably wide effect, not only on financial markets but also on the overall economy. Tackling these issues is an elusive task. However, they are central to the Colombian reality, and no analysis of the country would be complete without mentioning them briefly.

First, security issues in Colombia have been so intense and widespread that a clear majority of investors are very cautious about disclosing financial information. Entrepreneurs often give this reason for avoiding public capital markets. Although progress on the security front is evident, the deep institutional transformation that the country has undergone over the last 16 years will take time to reach and positively impact the mindset of the average private investor. Besides, further progress is required on many fronts, and the tangible benefits of the latest developments (for example, the 2016 peace accord with the rebels) have yet to fully unfold.

Second, the generational shift in entrepreneurs' families has begun, even among the largest, most traditional conglomerates. Second and third generations of management teams are returning from postgraduate studies in top universities around the world and successful careers abroad, feeding talent into corporate Colombia. In some cases, this transition is taking place with remarkable smoothness. The increasing openness, interest in international growth, focus on ESG standards, and better understanding of the benefits of capital markets have become evident and are much more common than they were only 5 or 10 years ago.

CONCLUSION

Developing capital markets in Colombia is a constant, demanding endeavor that requires work on many fronts. Still, there are plenty of reasons for optimism. The private sector, institutional framework, investor community, and regulatory authorities have worked together to achieve impressive progress. Continuous attention to seemingly smaller issues, such as those mentioned in this article, is likely to advance the long-term goal of developing well-structured and liquid capital markets that serve their economic purpose of boosting growth and providing prosperity.

5. Financial and Capital Market Developments in Mexico

Jorge Unda, CFA

To understand the Mexican capital markets, one must understand Mexico's deep economic crises, dramatic changes in the structure of the financial sector, and ideological political changes. The history of Mexico's capital markets also contains a series of effort to modernize, open, and reform the financial system.

The 1960s and 1970s marked real advances in the securities market in Mexico, starting with the issue of government short-term notes called CETES (Certificados de la Tesoreria) and *petrobonos* (oil price-linked government bonds) to finance internal debt. By 1969, the first steps were taken toward what would be the Ley del Mercado de Valores (Securities Exchange Law), which regulated all topics related to securities issuance—participants in the market, transparency, liquidity, transactions, and so forth. The law was finally approved in 1975. In 1978, the first security index linked to the Mexican stock market, the IPC (Índice de Precios y Cotizaciones), was established.[38]

THE CRISES OF THE 1970S

The mid-1970s also gave rise to a series of economic crises that plagued the development of the Mexican capital markets. Then, in the early 1980s, one of the most severe economic crises hit Mexico: excessive external debt (approximately USD 60 billion), profound current and fiscal deficits, and hyperinflation. The stock exchanges, as well as real economic output, fell dramatically, as did trading volumes. Mexico ended up nationalizing the banking system, leaving bank stocks with no trading activity because the government now owned the banks. They represented a large portion of the stock exchange's market capitalization and trading volume.

After the 1980s crisis and during the so-called stabilization process— focused on reducing the external debt burden, inflation, and fiscal imbalances—the financial markets went through a deep transformation. Central banking laws changed, as did the laws governing financial system participants, such as commercial banks, mutual funds, insurance companies, and broker/dealers. This allowed for the advent of new financial

[38]Mexico has two stock exchanges: the Bolsa Mexicana de Valores, commonly known as Mexican Bolsa, Mexbol, or BMV, and the Bolsa Institucional de Valores (BIVA).

institutions, especially broker/dealers, that took the market share of the nationalized banks. The 1985 earthquake in Mexico City and the global stock market crash of 1987 led to further depreciation of the peso and GDP contraction.

Despite these problems, Mexico returned to the international capital markets in the early 1990s, issuing government bonds in Europe, the United States, and Japan. Foreign capital inflows reached as high as USD 4 billion per year. Changes in the stock exchange law focused on globalization and foreigners' participation. In April 1990, Mexico's new and very modern stock exchange building opened. Following these efforts to internationalize the market, the US Securities and Exchange Commission named the Mexican stock exchange (BMV) an extraterritorial market and American depositary receipts for Mexican shares were listed on the NYSE. Also, efforts to implement electronic trading were made at this point.

The process of privatizing the banking system started in 1991, and the government sold its banks for prices three or more times their book value—owing to the inexperience of the "new bankers" (in general, former firms of brokers and dealers). Subsequently, weak macroeconomic conditions led to the financial crisis of 1994.

THE TEQUILA CRISIS

The 1994 Tequila Crisis put the brakes on the capital markets' growth, but the Mexican economy recovered in a short period thanks to the then-recently signed North American Free Trade Agreement, which allowed the export sector to grow nearly 100% in the six years after the crisis. Even though the Tequila Crisis reduced the volume and depth of the capital market, financial institutions and regulators continued improving their efficiency and expanding. They launched a series of instruments and developed new markets in the 1990s.

To understand the evolution of Mexico's financial system, one must first understand some of its political and economic aspects. Private banks were nationalized in 1982 because of political and ideological views and to manage the capital flows out of the country. The argument was that these outflows were not linked to the leverage levels and the country's fiscal weakness, both of which were related to the fall in oil prices. This crisis was of such magnitude that by August 1982, the country had failed to comply with its credit commitments. The following events of 1982 led to the nationalization of the banks.

1. February: A sharp decline in international reserves causes a depreciation of the peso.

2. August: The minister of finance reports that Mexico cannot cover its debt service. The US Federal Reserve and the US government award Mexico USD 3.5 billion.

3. September: The Mexican government nationalizes the banks to prevent the collapse of the financial system and imposes strong foreign exchange controls.

4. August through December: The peso is devalued 50%, interest rates soar to more than 100%, and the economy falls into a recession.

This crisis concluded in October 1985 with the Baker Plan, launched at the International Monetary Fund/World Bank meeting in Seoul, South Korea, by US Secretary of the Treasury James Baker. The Baker Plan specified that countries with high levels of indebtedness would have access to credit for the medium term in exchange for structural reforms. In 1984, the Paris Club, representing the creditor countries, carried out the restructuring of Mexican debt. In 1989, the Mexican government and creditor banks managed the restructuring of USD 49 billion of external debt.

Subsequent structural reforms were based on privatization of public enterprises, industrial deregulation, and liberalization of foreign investment, together with strong fiscal and monetary restraints.

For the financial system, these moves arguably began the liberalization of the market. Ceilings on bank deposits were eliminated, compulsory allocation of credit to certain sectors was removed, and subsidies were reduced. Financial reform was delayed, however, and the sector remained without proper supervision and regulation, a condition that would become evident in the 1994 Tequila Crisis.

An overview of the bank privatization process and the condition of the financial system during the Tequila Crisis and its subsequent resolution help explain the current banking system. From 1987 to 1994, the financial system achieved some reforms. These included the liberalization of interest rates, the end of credit controls, and the reduction of excessive reserve requirements. During this period, and after a lengthy process of austerity, credit growth was close to 50% a year. The exchange rate was fixed. High interest rates prevailed despite large capital inflows, mainly because of the growth in aggregate demand and the need to control inflation.

The most obvious causes of the crisis in 1994 were the high current account deficit, which was financed with short-term debt, overvaluation of the peso, and the disproportionate amount of US dollar-linked short-term debt. The speed of financial liberalization was likely another factor.

In the case of the newly privatized banks, two factors hampered success: (1) the lack of experience and the capability for credit analysis and (2) the lack of banking supervision—that is, the pretense that the reserve requirement was a sufficient regulatory condition, eliminating the need for supervision. After supervising only government-owned banks for over a decade, the regulatory agencies lacked the supervisory knowledge and experience needed to control the privatized banks.

Rapid growth of credit, expansionary monetary and fiscal policies, and rapid liberalization of the financial system have caused crises in several countries.[39] The excess of capital flows, the return of Mexico to the bond market in 1990, the euphoria caused by the substantial improvement in macroeconomic conditions, and their subsequent collapse helped deepen the external impact of the Tequila Crisis in 1994.

The Secretariat of Finance and Public Credit, along with external consultants—including Credit Suisse First Boston, McKinsey & Company, and Booz Allen Hamilton—privatized the Mexican banks through auctions starting in May 1990. The aim was to maximize the funds raised, but no information on valuations and assets was provided to inform the participating groups to help them understand the risks. This deficiency partly explains the high prices paid by the banks (the lowest price/book bid was 2.66×, and the highest was 5.3×).

The high prices paid for the banks, a growing economy, and a fixed exchange rate all caused strong credit growth. According to the Comisión Nacional Bancaria y de Valores (CNBV), an independent agency of the Secretariat of Finance and Public Credit, outstanding credit in current pesos went from MXN 180,000 million to MXN 800,000 million in just four years, representing 51% of GDP.[40] The banks also had to face the previous restructuring cost of FONAPRE (the Banking Fund for Preventive Aid, a fund created in 1984, managed by Banxico, and financed by the then-state-owned commercial banks) and FOBAPROA (the Banking Fund for Savings Protection).

In conclusion, the Tequila Crisis was caused by a series of events: continuous deterioration in the balance of payments and current account from 1990 to 1994 (–2.84%, –4.66%, –6.72%, –5.80%, and –7.05%, respectively, each year) and an increase in government and private short-term borrowing.[41] FOBAPROA insurance generated expectations for savers and bankers that increased the risk to banks, and regulatory weakness was evident. There was continued appreciation of the real exchange rate: According to Banxico, it touched levels below 70% of purchasing power parity on a 1990 basis. Also, banks' delinquency rates increased from 2.31% to 9.19% during this period (according to CNBV). All that finally led to the need for international support (mainly from

[39]Drees and Pazarbasioglu (1995).

[40]Hernández and Villagomez (2000).

[41]The balance of payments is expressed as a percentage of (in this case, Mexico's) GDP.

the United States) to bail out the country—a need that arose only 12 years after the previous sovereign debt default.

Only four years after 18 banks were privatized, the financial crisis forced a bailout of the banking system. The bailout consisted of establishing an institutional "dollar window" with the central bank, through which banks were able to access US dollars, the purchase of an asset portfolio through FOBAPROA promissory notes at rates equivalent to CETES (government short-term bills) plus a spread of 200 bps, shared loss contracts, and a capitalization commitment on the delinquent portfolio. Regulations forced an increase in reserves for default on nonperforming loans and a coverage ratio of 60% on the delinquent portfolio. Debtor rescue programs were in place for several years, and an inflation-linked unit (UDI) was created to lighten the burden of interests on mortgage credits.

The FOBAPROA debt became government debt in December 1998, and assets were transferred to the new Institute for Protection of the Bank Savings (Instituto de Protección al Ahorro Bancario, IPAB). The total fiscal cost as of 31 December 1999 corresponded to 19.3% of GDP, and the cost to be paid by IPAB had a net amount of 10.3% of GDP.

Finally, the structure of the banking system was transformed after the Tequila Crisis. In 1994, Mexico had 31 banks, including the privatized ones and new licenses. By 1999, the number had been reduced to 20, and from those originally sold in the privatization process, only 6 survived.

DEVELOPMENTS IN THE 21ST CENTURY

The 10 years following the Tequila Crisis and its aftermath brought major changes in Mexico's financial system and political and economic spheres. What might be called the birth of Mexican democracy began in 2000: An opposition party won the presidency, ousting the PRI (Partido Revolucionario Institucional), which had ruled since its creation in 1929.

Advances in the following years included the introduction of derivatives transactions and the creation of the MexDer Exchange for options and futures. By 1999, electronic trading was fully in place. In 2001, the first foreign stock was listed in Mexico and stock exchange certificates (*certificados bursátiles*, or CEBURES) were born in a new reform of the laws governing the stock exchange. The certificates were a way to finance private companies with long-term debt by issuing securities on the exchange. Also, the first global exchange-traded funds (ETFs) were listed in 2002, and in 2005, local ETFs and trackers were launched. In 2010, structured equity securities (*certificados de capital en desarrollo*, or CKDs) were created to attract Mexican pension funds to the private equity sector; in 2011, FIBRAs (*fideicomisos de inversión en bienes raíces*) were created for the same purpose, with FIBRAs giving pension funds access to real estate investment.

CAPITAL MARKETS EVOLUTION

The focus of this discussion now shifts to the development of the capital markets in Mexico from 2000 to 2016, a period marked by several structural changes.

1. The pension reform that changed public pensions from a defined-benefit to a defined-contribution structure gave birth to the Mexican private pension funds, the AFORES, which are private entities entitled to manage public pensions and which have long-term investment objectives.

2. The commitment of Banxico and the Mexican Treasury to creating a long-term government bond curve allowed investors to invest in bonds for the long term while also creating a benchmark for private long-term debt issuers.

3. Foreigners' participation in the local market created both liquidity and volume.

4. After the financial crisis, the consolidation and stabilization of private banks created an adequate environment for capital market securitization, project finance, and development of the debt capital market.

5. The fiscal and monetary authorities became committed to understanding macroeconomic prudence.

An important concern in the development of any emerging market is the crowding-out effect. To understand it, it is necessary to focus on the development of public debt in Mexico. From 2000 to 2016, total external debt went from USD 152 billion to USD 412 billion, roughly equivalent to 22% and 43% of GDP, respectively. Of the total external debt, public debt represented 54% in 2000 and 67% in 2016, growing from 12% to 30% of GDP. As a percentage of the total, then, the participation of private issuers has fallen, but this observation may be misleading because of the size of the increase in the amounts of external private debt, which went from USD 70 billion in 2000 to USD 133 billion in 2016. It seems at first glance, however, that public debt has been the main beneficiary of the growth of Mexican participation in the foreign capital markets.

As for the local market, in 2000, internal public debt represented 12.6% of GDP, but by 2015, this number had grown to 30%. The term structure of the debt changed dramatically in that period, however, and by 2015, almost 97% of the public internal debt was long term. In addition, 90% of the debt was issued in the local market, leading to the conclusion that the Mexican government has been a large issuer of long-term debt in the Mexican capital market. Who has been buying these securities? Mainly foreign investors. They started small in 2000, and their participation grew to a 7% share in 2004 and to more than 55% in 2016. In the same period, Mexican pension funds, mutual funds, and banks reduced their participation.

If the amount of government debt in the local market has increased dramatically, what has become of the private debt issuers? Has there been a crowding-out effect? To analyze this question, first note the evolution of the Mexican pension funds. In 2007, almost 10 years after their creation, their market capitalization equaled around 7% of GDP. In 2016, they represented close to 14% of GDP, and in Mexican pesos, their size increased 180%. At the same time, the share of government securities declined from roughly 63% to around 55% of total assets. Private issuers' share rose from 40% to almost 55%, and bank securities rose from 45% to 60% of total assets in the same period.

These facts lead to the conclusion that including Mexican bonds in 2013 in the World Government Bond Index (WGBI) prompted foreign investors to increase their participation in the local government debt market. This allowed other participants to reduce their participation in this type of security and provided room for private issuers and banks to participate in the local market.

The data for foreign investors and for Mexican pension funds greatly clarify the results and the change in market shares. For example, foreign holdings of local Mexican bonds went from MXN 92 billion in December 2005 to MXN 978 billion in December 2012 (before the country was included in the WGBI), then to MXN 1,140 billion in December 2013 (after entering the WGBI), and finally to MXN 1,810 billion in October 2017—an extraordinary growth rate. Meanwhile, Mexican pension funds grew from MXN 174 billion in December 2008 (after the pension reform) to MXN 304 billion in December 2012, then to MXN 339 billion in October 2017. From these numbers, the conclusion is that foreign participation helped local investors avoid the crowding-out effect from government debt issuance and allowed private and semi-private issuers to access long-term local markets.

CONCLUSION

An analysis of the private debt and equity securities in the local markets prompts a few conclusions. First, consider the profound change that happened in the issuances in the local equity market from 2000 to 2017. Pension reform was probably the main factor in this change. Local equity issuance over that period adds up to around USD 45.2 billion, but most of it has taken place since 2010. Of the total, 75% was issued between 2010 and 2017. In that seven-year period, a total of USD 34.2 billion was issued, which contrasts dramatically with the USD 11.2 billion issued from 2000 to 2010. Most of this more recent issuance was linked to real estate or the FIBRAs, the special real estate investment trust (REIT) created for AFORES that issued USD 11.8 billion in total, representing around 35% of total equity issued. Companies related to real estate, infrastructure, airports, and concessions invested USD 6.1 billion during the same time, with the remainder divided among other sectors.

Equity issuance by Mexican companies issuing in US dollars reached USD 11.2 billion, which represents only 25% of the amount issued in pesos (the USD 45.2 billion mentioned in the previous paragraph). This means that 75% of the total issues were peso denominated and 25% were dollar denominated. Thus, liquidity and the number of market participants have increased dramatically since the last decade. This phenomenon has two components: (1) the increase in local participation through local pension funds and (2) the increased willingness of foreigners to invest in local currency. Also, the inclusion of new asset classes, such as REITs, on the Mexican stock exchange has allowed not only an increase in diversification in the local market but also for the financing of infrastructure and real estate investments.

Finally, the financial reform of 2014 focused on improving the conditions of competition and the share of credit as a driver of economic growth. This process is part of a more flexible regulatory framework for banking and for modernization of the financial societies of multiple purpose (*sociedades financiera de objeto múltiple*, or sofomes), credit auxiliary activities (*organizaciones y actividades auxiliares de crédito*), and credit unions.

As part of the regulatory transformation, the development banks (*banca de desarrollo*) formed by nine governmental financial entities underwent these key changes:

1. redefinition of the mandate to goals of sustainability and efficient and prudent management of resources rather than the preservation of capital

2. greater power for the board of directors

3. improved human resources, with compensation based on effort and achievement of objectives

It is difficult to determine what will ultimately result from the financial reforms. Will they, as the Mexican government intends, create “more and cheaper credit”? Will they increase the growth rate of GDP by 0.5%? The problem is that it is difficult to separate the underlying growth trend, the impact of reform on economic growth, and the penetration of credit. Even more difficult is measuring the impact of the financial reforms by themselves. Also, as indicated by Moreno and Zamarripa (2014), two forces are in opposition: on the one hand, an expansionist policy and prudential regulation and, on the other hand, the difficulty and risks inherent in market penetration of entities whose regulation is not as exhaustive as in the case of banking credit—that is, the microfinance companies. Although one of the goals of the credit reforms has to do with reducing financial costs, for the supply side and the demand side, the financial reforms are expected to benefit consumers more. The aims are to support mobility of investments, make information less asymmetrical, encourage competition between banks, and reduce abusive practices and conditional sales in which institutions ask consumers to buy products to access credit. Also, development banks and the various agencies and institutions involved in the credit market must reduce legal costs in the implementation of guarantees and fees associated with the duration and feasibility of noncompliance processes. These changes will have a positive impact on the productive sectors, especially for small- and medium-sized enterprises, which until now have not participated in the credit market or have done so in a very limited way. A clear attempt is being made to make the development bank the main engine of this production sector. Finally, it is worth noting that since the financial reform was approved in 2014, credit penetration as a percentage of GDP has increased, reaching almost 35%. However, it is still difficult to differentiate inertia from reform improvements.

References

CEFP. *Cámara de Diputados.* Centro de Estudios de las Finanzas Públicas.

Drees, Burkhard, and Ceyla Pazarbasioglu. 1995. "The Nordic Banking Crises; Pitfalls in Financial Liberalization?" IMF Working Papers 95/61

FSB. 2012. "Identifying the Effects of Regulatory Reforms on Emerging Market and Developing Economies: A Review of Potential Unintended Consequences." Financial Stability Board report (19 June). www.fsb.org/2012/06/r_120619e/.

Hernández, Fausto, and Alejandro Villagómez. 2000. "La Estrutura de la Deuda em México." Inter-American Development Bank, Working Paper 123.

Moreno, Jorge O., and Guillermo Zamarripa. 2014. *Aspectos Económicos de la Reforma Financiera: Análisis y Reflexiones.* FUNDEF (Fundación de Estudios Financieros).

Telles, Marcelo. 2014. *Myths and Maths of Bancarization in Latam.* Credit Suisse.

Trillo, Fausto Hernández, and Omar Lopez Escarpulli. 2000. *Banking in Mexico, 1994–2000.* Centro de Investigación y Docencia Económicas.

6. Toward a Consolidated Emerging Market in Peru: A Historical Perspective

Melvin Escudero

The development of the Peruvian capital market has a relatively short history because a series of political and economic crises prevented its consolidation and emergence as we know it today. During the 1970s, a military government ruled Peru, implementing the nationalization of many companies and entire industries while introducing other left-leaning policies. In the 1980s, hyperinflation prevented the establishment of a minimum level of infrastructure necessary to allow equity and fixed-income markets to grow. During both decades, banks traditionally financed productive activity (in both public and private companies). Important state intervention with direct subsidies to different economic sectors consolidated the dominance of banking and the government as the most important financing agents.

Between 1992 and 1996, a new approach to economic development brought new estate regulations based on the free market and respect for private property. These enabled the emergence of a capital market that conforms to international standards and best practices. This conformity, in turn, promotes the free and open development of the capital market. In this gradual process of privatization, the state decided that the private sector should have control over the main capital market entities, such as the stock exchange, stock brokerage companies, securities depositories, credit rating agencies, custody entities, and market makers, among others. Furthermore, the state promulgated regulations for the new mutual fund industry (open-end funds), investment funds (closed-end funds), and securitization companies. Also, the new package of regulations allowed banks to establish their own stock brokerage houses, mutual fund managers, and trustee companies—and to engage in investment banking activities for structuring bond issues and initial public offerings. Under this institutional scheme, the Peruvian capital market has had relatively robust growth and development but remains far from fulfilling the initial hope of becoming an important financing platform for Peru, where banks control almost 90% of financing activity.

SUPPLY RESTRICTIONS

The business of financing Peruvian companies has become almost entirely private since the mid-1990s, with state financing oriented to public spending, public investment in infrastructure, and providing funds to agribusinesses. The state privatized all its development banks, except for the Banco de la Nación (which manages the treasury's money) and the agriculture bank. Privately owned banks represent a majority share of the aggregate financing of the economy and, in turn (because they control important retail distribution channels), also are the most important operators in the capital markets with their stock brokerage houses, mutual funds, and securitization companies.

Peruvian GDP growth in the last 27 years has averaged more than 5.5% per year, a rate reflecting a business boom at all levels and one not previously experienced in the country. This growth has helped reduce poverty levels from 60% to less than 20% of the population. The extraordinary progress is reflected in a huge rate of banking system growth that is without historical precedent. However, the capital market has shown more modest growth.

The following factors explain the slow growth in the supply of investment instruments in the Peruvian capital market:

1. Relatively rigid regulations in many cases have generated high costs as a result of excessive control, supervision, and bureaucracy. Also, in some cases, such regulations are outdated given advances in international markets.

2. The tax structure for capital market financing is uncompetitive compared with taxation of bank financing (in which all interest and capital gains are exempt from taxes, as opposed to capital markets financing).

3. The culture of bank financing, where banks have close commercial relationships with large, medium, and small companies, influences a considerable number of potential issuers of bonds and equities not to enter the capital market, reducing the potential supply of investment instruments.

4. The low level of financial sophistication of Peruvian companies prevents them from taking advantage of capital market opportunities where direct financing may be cheaper and the maturity might be longer than that offered by banks.

DEMAND RESTRICTIONS

Demand for local and international investments is essential for the development of any capital market. Diversified demand stimulates the issuance of financial products and, at the same time, creates liquidity and depth, attracting more investors. For this reason, promoting local demand (retail and institutional) is important to develop and attract significant foreign demand from international markets.

During the 1990s, the government promoted citizen participation by allowing citizens to participate in some of the privatizations. However, this experience had limited impact. Likewise, rising stock prices attracted waves of retail investors, but the sharp fall in prices in 1998–2002 and 2008–2009 discouraged a sizable number of these investors. These large fluctuations disappointed many conservative investors, who preferred the security of bank deposits despite their low long-term returns.

With the creation of institutional investors (private pension funds, insurance companies, and mutual funds) in Peru in the mid-1990s, significant growth in domestic demand was expected.

Private pension funds became the main source of domestic demand for stocks and bonds. Their rapid growth (they went from nothing to 30% of GDP in 23 years and currently have AUM of over USD 42 billion) allowed them to buy significant amounts of securities. This buying was positive for liquidity at the beginning, but over time, the continuous accumulation of capital (because the young population was primarily buying, not selling) reduced the float of the securities, lowering the liquidity of the markets. The evolving ability of Peruvian pension funds to invest abroad reduced price pressure in the local markets, with foreign investments making up 46% of pension funds' capital by 2017 as shown in **Figure 6.1.**

FIGURE 6.1. PERUVIAN PORTFOLIO-MANAGED PENSION FUNDS, 2008–2017

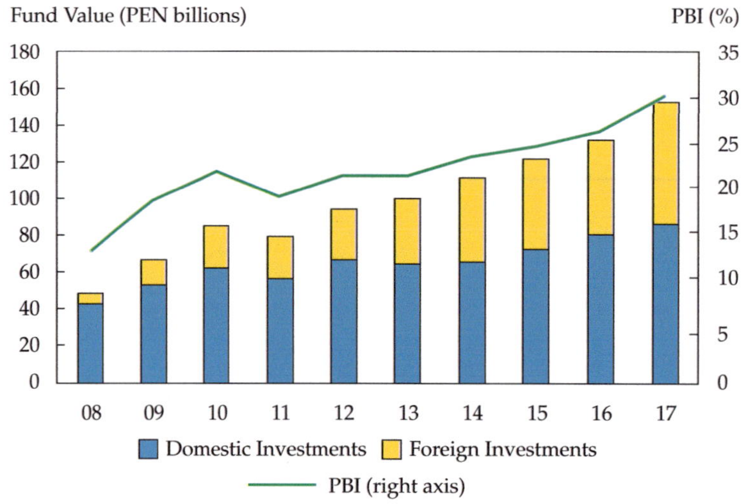

Note: 2017 data as of 30 November.

Source: Central Reserve Bank of Peru (BCRP).

The investments of insurance companies (which have USD 10 billion in AUM) have focused exclusively on the long-term fixed-income market. Insurance companies prefer bond issues between 5 and 30 years to maturity, and their investment in equity markets is very small. Likewise, mutual funds (USD 8 billion in AUM) mostly prefer debt instruments with short and medium terms to maturity (from one month to five years), with their investment in equities also being small (currently less than 10%).

The main problems on the demand side are the following:

1. A widespread lack of financial sophistication in the population that greatly inhibits needed flows from present and future retail investors

2. Families with high net worth, mostly owners of local companies, who have traditionally kept their surplus capital invested in international markets for diversification and protection

3. A tax system biased against the capital markets—bank instruments are tax exempt while capital market instruments are taxed at 30% on income and 5% on capital gains if they trade on the Lima Stock Exchange (Bolsa de Valores de Lima, or BVL)

4. A lack of diversity in demand, especially from local retail investors and from foreigners—many of the latter are discouraged because of the low liquidity and lack of depth in most equities listed on the BVL and in the whole fixed-income market

DUAL-CURRENCY ECONOMY

The hyperinflation of the second half of the 1980s, which reached levels of up to 40% per month, brought with it a deep fear of the currency losing its value, and the country ended up dollarizing the balance sheets of banks, companies, and families. The authorities allowed the free circulation of the US dollar. This situation remains in place, and the US dollar is currently accepted as a means of payment and store of value for savings. Dollarization of the economy has fallen from 80% at the beginning of the 1990s to less than 40% in 2017. This change, along with the opening of the Peruvian economy to the world, led to a significant volume of bond and stock issues in both currencies (US dollars and new soles). However, liquidity suffered as the securities were issued in both currencies In addition, the ability to issue securities and save in US dollars has enabled many companies and families to issue bonds and equities in the US market.

CURRENT STATUS OF THE PERUVIAN CAPITAL MARKET

In 2015, the BVL was put "under observation" by MSCI[42] to evaluate whether Peru, then classified as an "emerging market," should be classified as a "frontier market." (The frontier market designation is reserved for markets that are less developed than emerging markets.) The main reason for this cautionary step was the substantial drop in secondary liquidity, which was not enough to keep the market in the "emerging" category. One consideration was that the Peruvian stock market is regarded as dominated by mining. **Figure 6.2** shows that, effectively, between 35% and 55% of the weight of the general index has been in mining shares.

The drop in international prices of metals caused a corresponding decline in the prices and liquidity of mining shares. To avoid the downgrade classification from "emerging market" to "frontier market, a public–private effort was undertaken to promote the

FIGURE 6.2. SECTOR BREAKDOWN OF PERU'S STOCK MARKET CAPITALIZATION, 2005–2017

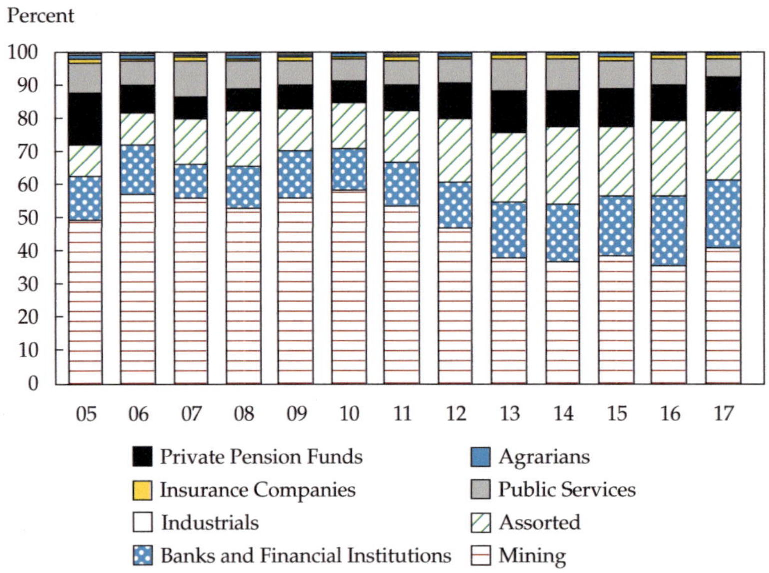

Source: BVL monthly report (2017).

[42]MSCI (Morgan Stanley Capital International) is a leading provider of investment decision support tools worldwide.

role of market makers, securities lending, automated trading, and the capital gains tax exemption for liquid stocks.

This effort was recognized, and MSCI maintained the category of emerging market for the BVL. With the rebound of the international prices of metals, the local mining stocks also rebounded. **Figures 6.3** and **6.4** show the increase in trading volume and stock market indexes during 2016 and 2017.

Despite these increases in prices and trading volume, the BVL continues to be considered illiquid, with a relatively low capitalization.

Figure 6.5 shows that although many companies are listed, only 10–20 have an acceptable level of liquidity. Most listed shares are illiquid because the number of listed companies is swelled by a law requiring all banks and insurance companies to be listed or because they have a tax advantage of 5% in capital gains (nonlisted stocks have capital gains taxed at 30%).

In the fixed-income market, sovereign bonds have a significant presence in the local and international markets. However, as can be seen from **Figure 6.6**, the total level

FIGURE 6.3. TRADED VALUE IN PERU'S STOCK EXCHANGE, 2003–2017

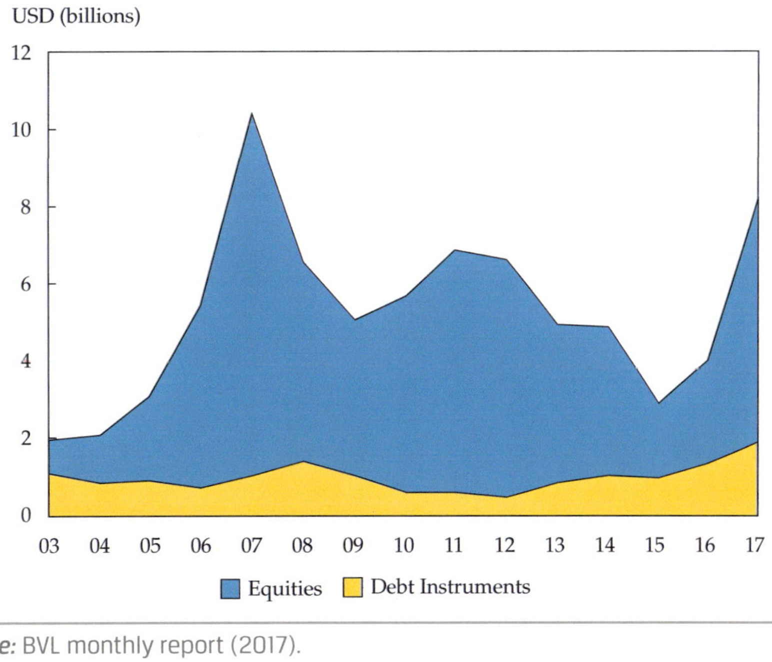

Source: BVL monthly report (2017).

FIGURE 6.4. PERFORMANCE OF PERU'S STOCK MARKET INDEXES, 2008–2017

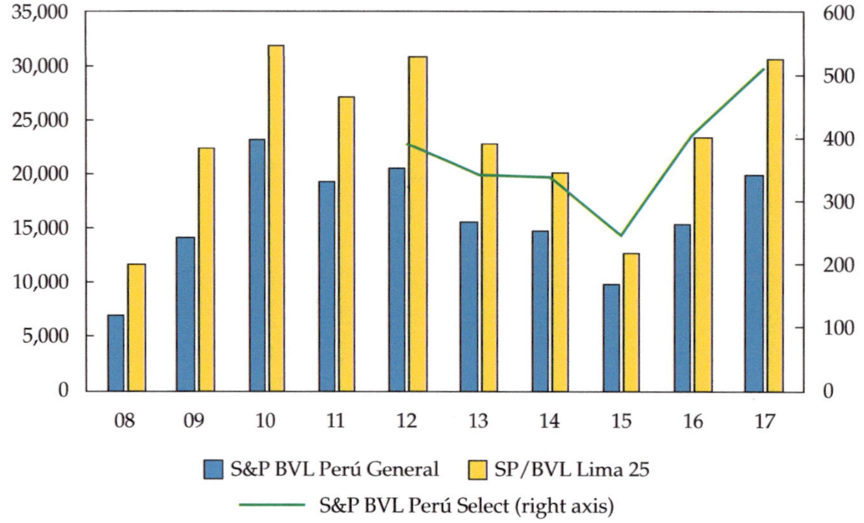

Source: BVL monthly report (2017).

FIGURE 6.5. TOTAL MARKET VALUE AND NUMBER OF LOCAL LISTED COMPANIES IN PERU, 2005–2017

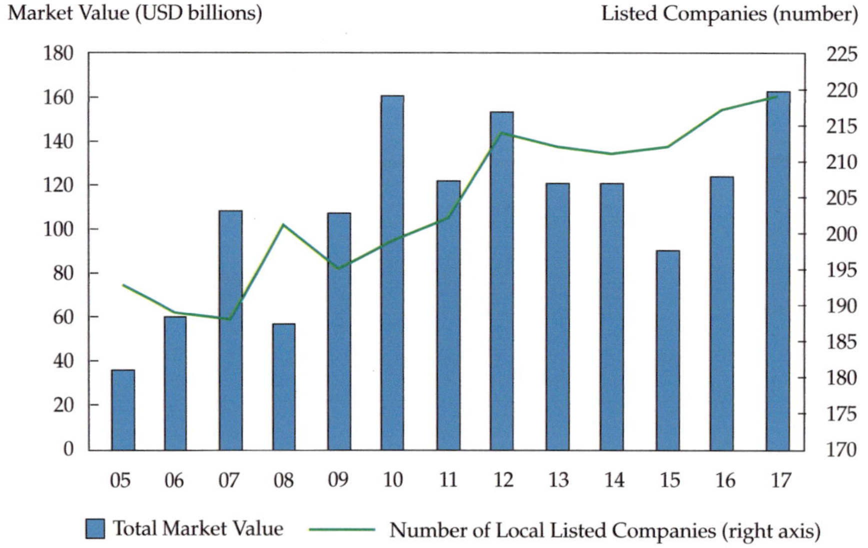

Source: BVL monthly report (2017).

FIGURE 6.6. PERU'S PUBLIC DEBT, 2003–2017

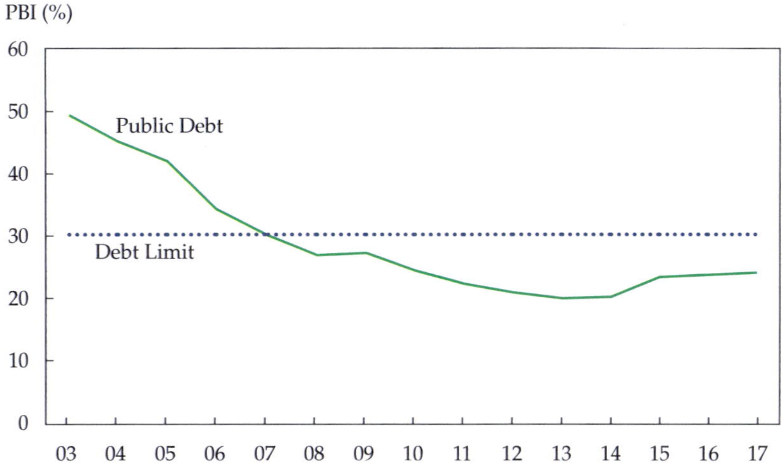

Note: 2017 data as of 30 November.

Source: Central Reserve Bank of Peru (BCRP).

of Peruvian debt (including bonds and credits with states and multilaterals) has been declining, reaching levels of 24% of GDP, below the legal maximum of 30% of GDP.

As a result, Peru's credit risk is between BBB+ and A–, according to the main international credit rating agencies. This international recognition of good Peruvian fiscal management has also been reflected in a significant drop in country risk. **Figure 6.7** shows a decreasing Emerging Markets Bond Index (EMBI)[43] spread for Peru, which ended 2017 below 100 bps—its lowest historical point in 10 years.

This turn of events makes Peruvian sovereign bonds among the safest in Latin America, very close to the level of Chilean bonds. However, the outlook in the issuance of private corporate bonds is not the same. In fact, issuance is relatively stagnant as, after a rebound in 2009 and 2012, recent years have shown low activity in the local market, as shown in **Figure 6.8**.

The predominance of bank lending and the decision of many issuers to place their bonds in international markets (mainly in the US market) explains the sluggishness of the bond market. In addition, the tendency of bond investors to "buy and hold" until maturity, because of excess demand for the bonds, leads to a secondary market that is almost nonexistent because of the small number of transactions and float.

[43]The EMBI is the main country risk indicator, calculated by JPMorgan.

FIGURE 6.7. COUNTRY RISK (JPMORGAN EMBI+ PERU)

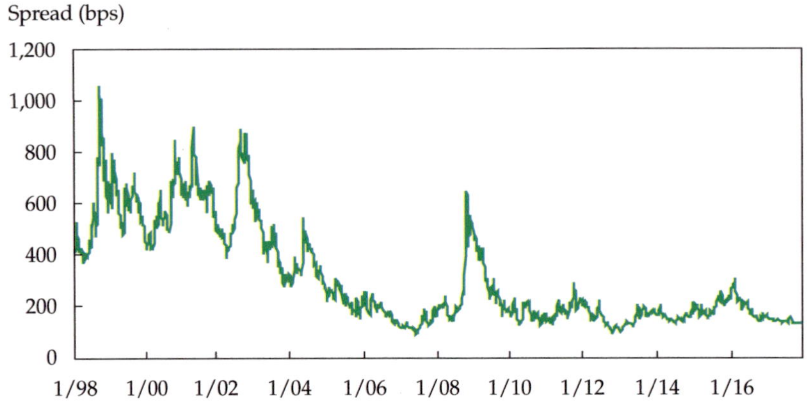

Note: Data as of 10 January 2018.

Source: Central Reserve Bank of Peru (BCRP).

FIGURE 6.8. CORPORATE BOND ISSUES, 2003–2017

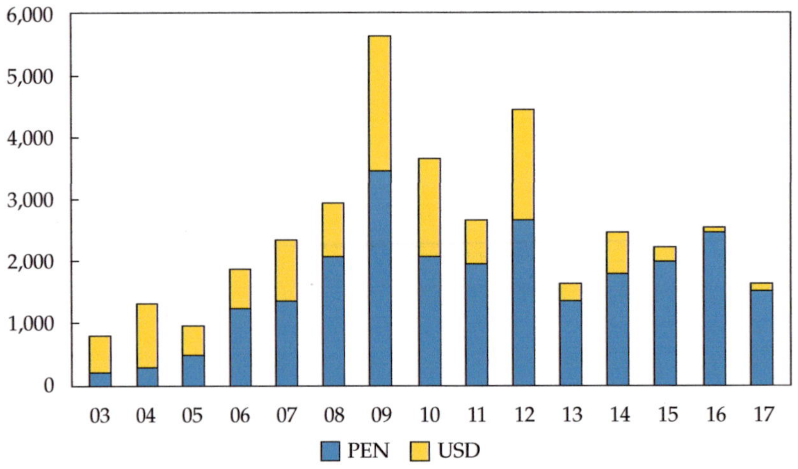

Note: 2017 data are as of 30 November.

Sources: Superintendence of the Stock Market (SMV) and the BCRP.

FUTURE CHALLENGES

The main goal of the Peruvian capital market is to create more liquidity and depth to stimulate the demand for, and supply of, securities and thus become an important alternative to traditional banking. In this regard, the financial culture of both the issuing companies and of retail and institutional investors must change. This effort is long term and should be promoted by the state and by the private sector.

In addition, regulators—the Ministry of Economy and Finance, the Superintendency of Securities Markets, and the Superintendency of Insurance, Banking and Private Pension Funds—must coordinate to reduce bureaucracy and eliminate bottlenecks that restrict the development of the capital market. They also must help the market to proactively introduce the best practices observed in international markets.

By following these prescriptions, the Peruvian capital market can become a regional financial hub in the medium term. It is the only country in the region that has allowed the creation of a multicurrency platform (securities can be issued in soles, US dollars, or any Latin American or international currency) and that maintains a free capital flow scheme and unrestricted local and foreign ownership of all the institutions participating in this market.

Likewise, the financial integration of the Pacific Alliance could bring important benefits. In July 2015, during the Pacific Alliance Summit organized in Peru, the second stage in the integration process between Mexico, Colombia, Peru, and Chile was announced by the four countries' finance ministers: financial integration, following the free trade agreement. With this announcement, the dream of building one of the 10 largest, most liquid, and deep capital markets in the world came closer to reality, reflecting the financial and business interests of the four countries, which represent 216 million people with an aggregate GDP over USD 2 trillion (close to the current size of Brazil).

To date, Peruvian capital markets have made important advances but still face great challenges in achieving a single, integrated financial platform that will provide the many benefits for markets, businesses, and citizens. First, unlike commercial integration, which seeks to eliminate or reduce impediments to free trade, financial integration is much more complex because it also implies influencing the internal regulation of each country, including the regulation of capital markets, financial markets, and tax treatment.

The current direction is the right one and includes mutual recognition of equities and fixed-income issues—securities issued in Pacific Alliance countries receive the same treatment and conditions as if they were locally issued—electronic integration of stock exchanges, and the joint announcements made in October 2017 by the four finance ministers. The finance ministers committed to implement the passport for fund managers (under which an operating license in one country would allow the fund manager to operate in the other three countries), the joint issuance of catastrophe bonds, the joint launch of an infrastructure fund, and the elimination of double taxation for private pension funds of the Pacific Alliance, putting a ceiling of 10% on the capital gains tax. Another measure that would have a positive impact on the flows is still pending at this writing: The local investment limit for private pension funds will apply to all investments made in the four countries of the Pacific Alliance.

If the Pacific Alliance integration process continues to move forward, several of the limitations of the Peruvian capital market, especially its small size and low liquidity, will soon be a bad memory. The Peruvian market would benefit through integration because it would gain scale, volume, greater negotiation and liquidity, and greater diversification of both investment instruments and types of investors.

References

Banco Central de Reserva del Perú. 2017. "*Series Estadísticas*" (December). https://estadisticas.bcrp.gob.pe/estadisticas/series/.

BVL. 2017. *Boletín Diario* (December). www.bvl.com.pe/merc_publi_boletindiario.html.

BVL. 2017. *Informe Bursátil* (December). www.bvl.com.pe/pubdif/infmen/Ultimo_IB.pdf.

Superintendencia de Mercado de Valores. 2017. *Reporte Mensual* (December). www.smv.gob.pe/Frm_RptMensual.aspx?data=2BCE27555D2CC9E798E7AB5F0DD3507E22252404EF.

7. Uruguay: A Small Market with a Tradition of Trust

Barbara Mainzer, CFA

INTRODUCTION

Uruguay, one of the smallest countries in South America in terms of territory (176,215 km^2) and population (3.29 million inhabitants), is well known for its stability and for an open and trustworthy financial system. Situated in a volatile region, Uruguay is seen as a bastion of institutional and social stability, with a solid democracy where the rule of law is respected equally for citizens and foreigners. Because of its stable political system, egalitarian society, highly educated population, and strong financial sector, Uruguay earned the nickname the "Switzerland of the Americas" in the 1950s.

Uruguay's financial model is based on broad financial freedom with no limitations on capital flows. This, combined with its solid democracy and a predictable economic policy regardless of the party in power, has made Uruguay the offshore financial center chosen by affluent and high-net-worth investors; many international financial institutions have selected it as the hub for their branch offices and representations.

THE URUGUAYAN WAY

Uruguay takes pride in keeping its international commitments and has not defaulted on its sovereign debt in its modern history. The country has shown its resolve to honor its promises despite seemingly overwhelming internal and external pressures. The most recent example was the 2002–03 financial crisis. At that time, the country lost 50% of its deposits and the economy contracted almost 8% in one year and 15% from peak to trough (from 1998 to 2002).

After the amortization of a bond in February 2003, reserves were below the technical minimum and continued to dwindle because of deposit withdrawals. Negotiations for a debt restructuring finished three months later, resulting in an agreement with creditors to extend the maturity of the debt but with no haircut. Holdouts, accounting for 7% of total debt, received their payments as originally scheduled. This strengthened the country's reputation and allowed it to tap the international capital market again a few months later, with the issuance of a local currency inflation-linked bond; over the next several years, Uruguay significantly improved its debt profile through an active management of its liabilities.

THE RIGHT STEPS

Since 2003, Uruguay's government has taken a more strategic approach to managing its debt, as shown in **Figure 7.1**. It has moved to de-dollarize and extend its maturity. In addition, it has reduced the percentage of floating-rate debt and broadened and diversified its investor base. These changes have allowed Uruguay to significantly reduce its refinancing risk, the negative effects of a potential depreciation of the peso, and its interest rate risk. Furthermore, the liquidity of government debt has increased and the sovereign yield curves that serve as a reference for the rest of the issuers were constructed.

The country regained its investment-grade rating in April 2012. Today, Uruguay is one of five Latin American countries with investment-grade ratings from all three major rating agencies. It is also at the top of the ranking of emerging markets by transparency and quality of information published by the Institute for International Finance.

FIGURE 7.1. IMPROVEMENT IN URUGUAY'S DEBT PROFILE, 2004–2017

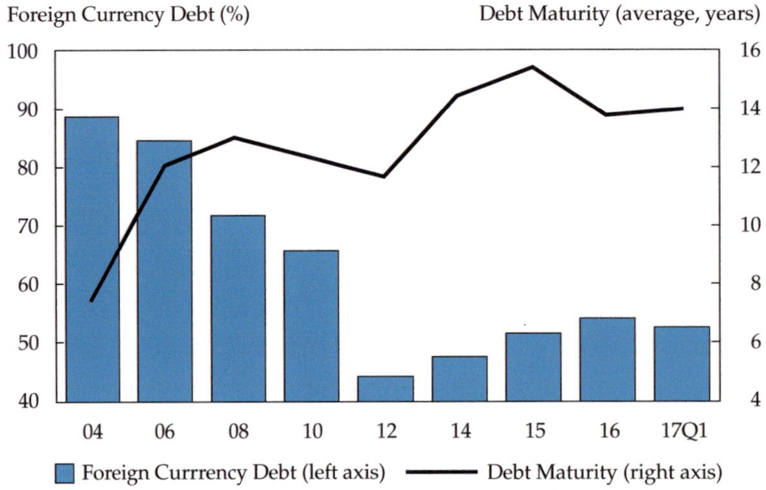

Source: Uruguayan Debt Management Unit.

THE URUGUAYAN BANKING SYSTEM

Between 2002 and 2016, the Uruguayan economy had the longest economic expansion on record. By 2016, the gross domestic product was about USD 52.4 billion, implying a per capita GDP of USD 15,620, which is consistent with its World Bank classification as an Upper Income Economy and sets it apart as one of the highest-income economies of its region.

Growth, coupled with prudent measures taken by the government and the regulator, has set the foundation for the country's sound, stable, and transparent financial system. Regulatory adjustments have included increasing the prudence ratios and lowering the liquidity and exchange rate risk of the banks.

The banking system has been consolidating over the last decades. Eleven banks operate in the country; two are government owned and nine are private. This consolidation is partly explained by the high costs and increasing regulations that the banking industry faces, with subsequent low returns for bank shareholders.

The banking sector is highly concentrated both by loan issuance and by deposits received, as shown in **Figure 7.2**. Government-owned banks have a preponderant role, with the BROU (Banco de la República Oriental del Uruguay) standing out as the clear market leader.

The banking system plays a preponderant role in financial intermediation and is the dominant player in the money market. The system also has the largest spreads between

FIGURE 7.2. URUGUAY LOANS AND DEPOSITS

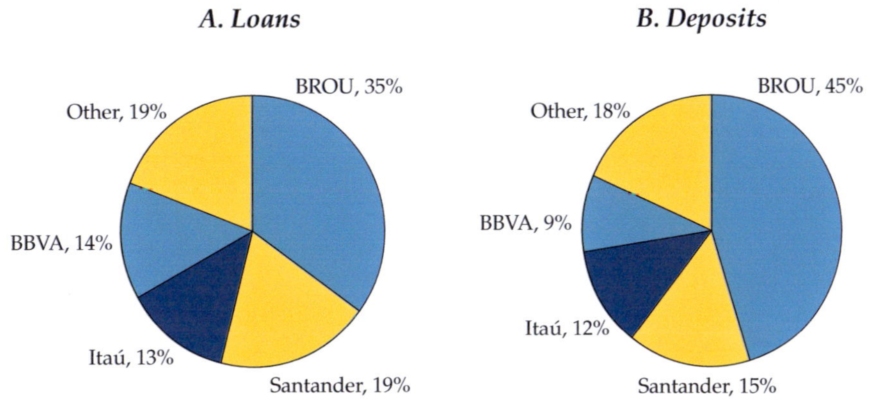

Source: Author's calculations with Central Bank of Uruguay (BCU) data as of 31 December 2016.

lending and deposit rates in the world, which, among other issues, makes the interest rate transmission channel of monetary policy somewhat ineffective at conveying signals correctly to the rest of the economy. **Figure 7.3** shows the market's interest rate spread.

THE URUGUAYAN CAPITAL MARKETS

In a region where capital markets tend to be less developed, Uruguay's capital market stands out as less dynamic and less innovative, despite the country having the highest per capita income in Latin America,[44] the lowest return on deposits, and a long-established centralized stock exchange (the Sociedad de Bolsa Montevideana was created in 1867 and is the precursor of the Uruguayan stock exchange, the BVM). Numerous studies analyzing the lag of the Uruguayan capital markets compared with those of other countries have examined such factors as the small size of companies, low level of sophistication of the various actors, the 2002 and 2008 financial crises, macro aspects, corporate governance issues, and institutional and regulatory weaknesses, among others.

FIGURE 7.3. NOMINAL PESO INTEREST RATE SPREAD, 2008–2017

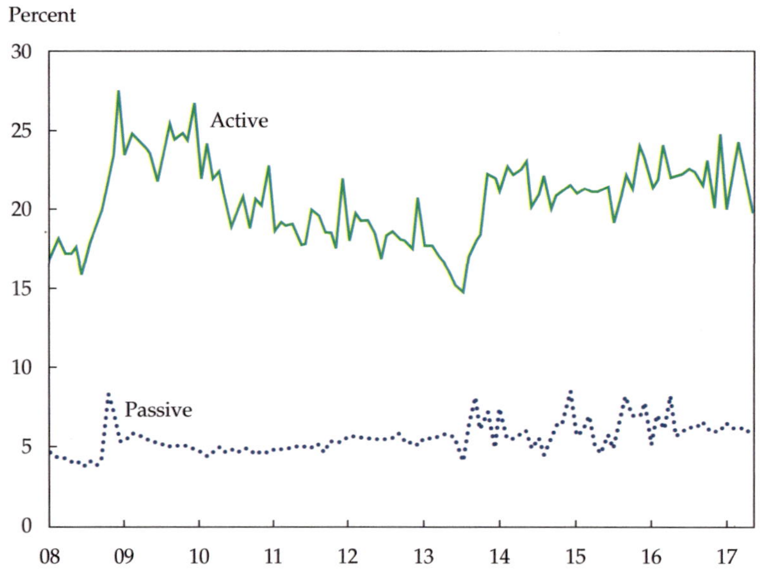

Source: Author's calculations with BCU data as of 30 June 2017.

[44]As of 2017, it was the highest in nominal terms, but Chile was higher in PPP terms.

The equity market is very small and illiquid. Despite recent growth, equity market cap is 1.8% of GDP, a figure that is low even when compared with other smaller and less developed Latin American countries, such as Bolivia (20%), El Salvador (76%), and Paraguay (4.7%). Private debt market capitalization is also very small, at 3.7% of GDP, and illiquid, whereas bank deposits and public debt represent 48% and 55% of GDP, respectively. Local companies continue to fund themselves with bank loans, retained earnings, or supplier credit.

Although the market for corporate debt has always been relatively small, it saw a significant increase in activity in the mid-1990s, with almost 20 corporate bond issues per year in 1996 and 1997. A fraud led to a high-profile default in 1998, and the resulting crisis led to about half the issuers either restructuring or defaulting on their debt. The market went into a decline from which it only began to recover in the mid-2000s.

Corporate bond issuance has recently seen a renaissance as the result of the development of special purpose vehicles (SPVs), specifically financial trusts (*fideicomisos financieros*). SPVs for financing agricultural activities, construction, and energy have been very popular and well received. A study by República AFAP shows that more than 64% of the private sector issuance between 2004 and 2016 corresponded to SPVs—40% corresponded to debt instruments and 60% corresponded to *instrumentos de participación* (proxies to equities).

Another distinctive feature of the Uruguayan capital markets is the predominance of the primary market over the secondary market. The small size of the secondary market is due to two factors. First, the Central Bank of Uruguay implements monetary policy by issuing its own short-term bills in the primary market, while most central banks implement monetary policy using repos backed by government securities. Second, many investors tend to implement a buy-and-hold strategy, which reduces secondary market liquidity.

The main debt issuer is the government, with a weighting of more than 90%. Its securities are the most liquid and the most heavily traded in the formal secondary market.

Each of the three reference currencies has its own sovereign curve. The deepest and most liquid one is in US dollars, with original issues of up to 36 years and a relatively tight sovereign spread versus US Treasuries. Most of the bonds that make up this curve are constituents of major emerging market sovereign debt indexes. The market in inflation-linked units (UIs) is also deep, with original issues of up to 30 years. Some of these were issued in the international markets as adjustable US dollar bonds with exposure to UIs. Finally, the nominal peso (UYP) curve is composed of bonds originally issued with up to a five-year maturity. In June 2017, in an event considered a milestone for local and international financial markets, the country issued, in the international markets, its first five-year bond in Uruguayan pesos. The issue, for USD 1,250 million, was almost four times oversubscribed, with a diversified investor base, and was included in the JPMorgan Government Bond Index-Emerging Markets.

Private pension funds are the largest institutional investors. The four pension funds (Administrators of Pension Savings Funds, or AFAPs) have USD 16 billion in AUM (30% of GDP). Although they basically exercise a buy-and-hold strategy, they are active in the spot market, constituting an important source of market liquidity and helping the price discovery process. Furthermore, they are critically important for financing the government's liquidity needs because they invest around 70% of their funds in government bonds. They played a central role during the 2002–03 crisis, when they were almost the only buyers in the market.

One regulator bears the responsibility of regulating and supervising all financial institutions and markets: the Central Bank of Uruguay. Even though most agree that increased regulation does contribute to protecting the financial system from unforeseen shocks, market participants consider compliance quite costly.

Despite the tiny size of its capital market, Uruguay has two stock exchanges: Bolsa Electrónica de Valores (BEVSA) and Bolsa de Valores de Montevideo (BVM). BEVSA is primarily used by wholesale traders and institutional investors, while BVM caters more to retail investors. The largest exchange by trading volume is BEVSA, which is organized into three markets: exchange, money, and asset markets (primary and secondary).

In addition to this formal, transparent, and centrally organized market, a large and thriving OTC market exists. Its size is unknown, but all private estimates indicate that it is significant. The BVM asks its members to declare the amount of assets traded away from formal markets. Although the total cap of assets traded in formal markets in 2014 was USD 1.1 billion, the total cap of assets traded in this part of the OTC market was nine times larger, or USD 9.5 billion. Another indication of the size of the OTC market is the number of independent registered advisers: 149, with several more in the process of requesting a license.

Uruguay has a large number of securities intermediaries. If all agents are considered (stock brokers in BVM and BEVSA, securities agents and registered investment advisers), there are more than 200. Dunn (2015) estimates this figure at 72 in Bovespa (São Paulo Stock Exchange), 102 in the Santiago Stock Exchange, and 96 in Mexico.

AN OFFSHORE FINANCIAL HUB

Montevideo was for decades one of the hubs chosen by high-net-worth investors as well as middle-class Argentineans and Brazilians looking to protect their wealth, keeping it safe from populist governments, shaky banking systems, heavy-handed tax authorities, and potential kidnappers. In the 1990s and early 2000s, populist governments and harsher rules and regulations in such countries as Brazil and Argentina led large institutions to reassess their strategy and move out of these countries in favor of more stable and business-friendly hubs like Uruguay. During the early 2000s, Uruguay had branch offices of, among others, Merrill Lynch, UBS, Credit Suisse, Prudential (then Wachovia), Royal Bank of Canada, and Santander Private Banking. The 2008 financial crisis and increased regulations forced many large institutions to again reassess their strategy and in many cases retreat from the region back to their core markets. Since then, many firms have closed their operations in the country, including BNP Paribas, Societe Generale, Crédit Lyonnais, Credit Uruguay, Royal Bank of Canada, UBS Switzerland, Wells Fargo, Merrill Lynch, Bank Leumi, and recently, the representative offices of Credit Suisse, Bank Hapoalim, and Bank Mizrahi-Tefahot.

The landscape continues to evolve with the emergence of competition from, among others, the large networks of independent financial advisers and multifamily offices.

URUGUAY'S CAPITAL MARKETS: THE ROAD AHEAD

Uruguay is a small country without a local capital market culture or large companies. Developing capital markets will not be an easy task. The capital market has always been, and will probably always be, a fixed-income market.

The country has several strengths upon which it can build: a longstanding tradition of trust, strong and respectable institutions, and political and economic stability. Because it has the highest per capita income in Latin America and the lowest real return for deposits, it also has a potential investor base keen for alternatives and higher return.

The Financial Inclusion Law, enacted in 2014, encourages the population to make larger use of the financial system's tools. This, in turn, will encourage financial intermediaries and issuers to develop instruments targeted to this segment. Money market funds denominated in pesos have been created and strategic alliances have been established to distribute products targeted for the small investor.

Furthermore, the government has established a commission dedicated to promoting the capital markets, tasked with setting up a plan to develop these markets. This commission, integrated by key participants of the government as well as the private financial sector, has the potential to make significant contributions if given the right attention and powers.

Private pension funds have a large and growing pool of resources they need to invest—and they are willing to invest in the private capital market sector if they are presented with adequate opportunities.

SPVs could contribute to making the local capital markets more dynamic. These vehicles are not only easier to structure but also allow smaller companies to tap the capital markets (through cash flow bundling). They can also be structured with equity-like characteristics. In this way, one of the weaknesses of the Uruguayan capital market (the small size of its companies) can be overcome. Dunn (2015) expects that, as occurred in such other countries in the region as Ecuador and Bolivia, the Uruguayan capital market's growth will come from SPVs.

In addition, the Public-Private Participation (PPP) program, regulated by a 2011 law, could also contribute to making local capital markets more dynamic as well as having a positive effect on the long-term growth of Uruguay's economy. Under this scheme, public and private institutions enter into a cooperative arrangement for the provision of a public service, typically with a long-term nature. The implementation has been slow but seems to be picking up.

Several measures are currently being implemented, and further steps will likely be taken at some point along the road to capital market development. Increasing financial literacy levels is key so that investors—and citizens in general—can make informed decisions. Attempts are being made to unify both stock exchanges and to continue working toward more-integrated regional stock markets to improve market depth and liquidity—which is in line with international evidence toward stock exchange consolidation. Efforts are being made to expand the population's access to such instruments as money markets and facilitate and reduce market access costs while introducing a more efficient approval process for new issues.

Uruguay has many characteristics to be proud of: It is a country where laws, regulations, and contracts are fully respected and transparency and access to information are valued and promoted. To thrive in the new global environment of increased financial transparency and more-efficient regulation, Uruguay can build on its strengths and work toward reducing inefficiencies and transaction costs.

References

Demirgüc-Kunt, A., and R. Levine. 1999. "*Bank-Based and Market-Based Financial System: Cross Country Comparisons.*" World Bank Development Research Group, Finance (July).

Dunn, Jaime. 2015. "*Diagnóstico General del Mercado de Valores Formal de Uruguay*" (16 April). www.scribd.com/document/327241240/DIAGNOSTICO-GENERAL-DEL-MERCADO-DE-VALORES-FORMAL-DE-URUGUAY-Jaime-Dunn.

Federal Reserve Bank of San Francisco. 2005. "*Please Explain How Financial Markets May Affect Economic Performance*" (January). www.frbsf.org/education/publications/doctor-econ/2005/january/financial-markets-economic-performance/.

Gray, Simon, and Nick Talbot. "Developing Financial Markets." *Handbooks in Central Banking No. 26*, CCBS, Bank of England.

Hawkins, John. 2001. "Bond Market and Banks in Emerging Economies." BIS Background Paper (December). www.bis.org/publ/bppdf/bispap11d.pdf.

Jiménez, Luis Felipe, and Sandra Manuelito. 2011. "*América Latina: Sistemas Financieros y Financiamiento de la Inversión. Diagnósticos y Propuestas.*" Revista CEPAL N° 103 (April). https://repositorio.cepal.org/handle/11362/11448.

Sundararajan, V. 2003. "Financial Market Development: Sequencing of Reforms to Ensure Stability." Paper presented at Fifth Annual Financial Markets and Development Conference organized by Brookings Institution, the IMF, and the World Bank, Washington, DC (14 April).

Tumpel-Gugerell, Gertrude. 2003. "The Role of Institutions in the Financial System." Center for Financial Stability, European Central Bank (November). www.ecb.europa.eu/press/key/date/2003/html/sp031111.en.html.

Uruguay, X.X.I. 2014. "*Informe Sistema Financiero: Promoción de Importaciones y Exportaçiones*" (April). www.uruguayxxi.gub.uy/inversiones/wp-content/uploads/sites/3/2014/09/Informe-Sistema-Financiero-Abril-2014_URUGUAYXXI.pdf.

Williams, Aime. 2016. "Millenials Set to Embrace Micro-Investing." *Financial Times* (17 June). www.ft.com/content/080de85e-3176-11e6-ad39-3fee5ffe5b5b.

Named Endowments

The CFA Institute Research Foundation acknowledges with sincere gratitude the generous contributions of the Named Endowment participants listed below.

Gifts of at least US$100,000 qualify donors for membership in the Named Endowment category, which recognizes in perpetuity the commitment toward unbiased, practitioner-oriented, relevant research that these firms and individuals have expressed through their generous support of the CFA Institute Research Foundation.

Ameritech
Anonymous
Robert D. Arnott
Theodore R. Aronson, CFA
Asahi Mutual Life Insurance Company
Batterymarch Financial Management
Boston Company
Boston Partners Asset Management, L.P.
Gary P. Brinson, CFA
Brinson Partners, Inc.
Capital Group International, Inc.
Concord Capital Management
Dai-Ichi Life Company
Daiwa Securities
Mr. and Mrs. Jeffrey Diermeier
Gifford Fong Associates
Investment Counsel Association of America, Inc.
Jacobs Levy Equity Management
John A. Gunn, CFA
Jon L. Hagler Foundation
Long-Term Credit Bank of Japan, Ltd.
Lynch, Jones & Ryan, LLC
Meiji Mutual Life Insurance Company
Miller Anderson & Sherrerd, LLP
John B. Neff
Nikko Securities Co., Ltd.
Nippon Life Insurance Company of Japan
Nomura Securities Co., Ltd.
Payden & Rygel
Provident National Bank
Frank K. Reilly, CFA
Salomon Brothers
Sassoon Holdings Pte. Ltd.
Scudder Stevens & Clark
Security Analysts Association of Japan
Shaw Data Securities, Inc.
Sit Investment Associates, Inc.
Standish, Ayer & Wood, Inc.
State Farm Insurance Company
Sumitomo Life America, Inc.
T. Rowe Price Associates, Inc.
Templeton Investment Counsel Inc.
Frank Trainer, CFA
Travelers Insurance Co.
USF&G Companies
Yamaichi Securities Co., Ltd.

Senior Research Fellows

Financial Services Analyst Association

For more on upcoming Research Foundation publications and webcasts, please visit www.cfainstitute.org/learning/foundation.

Research Foundation monographs are online at www.cfapubs.org.

CFA INSTITUTE RESEARCH FOUNDATION CONTRIBUTION FORM

☑ **Yes**, I want CFA Institute Research Foundation to continue to fund innovative research that advances the investment management profession. Please accept my tax-deductible contribution at the following level:

Thought Leadership Circle .... US$1,000,000 or more
Named Endowment .... US$100,000 to US$999,999
Research Fellow .... US$10,000 to US$99,999
Contributing Donor ....US$1,000 to US$9,999
Friend .... Up to US$999
I would like to donate US$____________________.

☐ My check is enclosed (payable to CFA Institute Research Foundation).
☐ I would like to donate appreciated securities (send me information).
☐ Please charge my donation to my credit card.

☐ VISA ☐ MC ☐ Amex ☐ Diners

Card Number

__ __ / __ __ ____________________

Expiration Date Name on card PLEASE PRINT

☐ Corporate Card
☐ Personal Card ____________________

Signature

☐ This is a pledge. Please bill me for my donation of US$ ____________
☐ I would like recognition of my donation to be:
☐ Individual donation ☐ Corporate donation ☐ Different individual

____

PLEASE PRINT NAME OR COMPANY NAME AS YOU WOULD LIKE IT TO APPEAR

PLEASE PRINT ☐ Mr. ☐ Mrs. ☐ Ms. MEMBER NUMBER____________

Last Name (Family Name) First (Given Name) Middle Initial

Title

Address

City State/Province Country ZIP/Postal Code

Please mail this completed form with your contribution to:
CFA Institute Research Foundation • P.O. Box 2082
Charlottesville, VA 22902-2082 USA

For more on CFA Institute Research Foundation, please visit www.cfainstitute.org/learning/foundation/Pages/index.aspx.

Made in the USA
Monee, IL
05 November 2026

67378077R00057